Women and Soldiers

*Sexual Violence and Survival Strategies
in Occupied Japan*

Women and Soldiers

Sexual Violence and Survival Strategies in Occupied Japan

By

Toshimi Chazono

Translated by
Tomoko Aoyama, Penny Bailey, Barbara Hartley,
Helen Kilpatrick, Mariko Kishi-Debski, Akiko Uchiyama
and Judy Wakabayashi

TRANS
PACIFIC
PRESS

Women and Soldiers: Sexual Violence and Survival Strategies in Occupied Japan
© Toshimi Chazono, 2024
Originally published in 2018, *Mou hitotsu no senryou* (Another Occupation)
by Inpakuto Shuppankai.
This English edition published in 2024 by Trans Pacific Press Co., Ltd.

Trans Pacific Press Co., Ltd.
PO Box 8547
#19682
Boston, MA, 02114, United States
Phone: +1-6178610545
Email: info@transpacificpress.com
Web: http://www.transpacificpress.com

Translated by Tomoko Aoyama, Penny Bailey, Barbara Hartley, Helen Kilpatrick,
Mariko Kishi-Debski, Akiko Uchiyama and Judy Wakabayashi

Copyedited by Miriam Riley, Armidale, NSW, Australia
Layout designed and set by Ryo Kuroda, Tsukuba-city, Ibaraki, Japan
Cover designed by Klassic Designs
Artworks on the first page of each chapter and on the back cover by Nobuko Willis.

Distributors

USA, Canada and India
Independent Publishers Group (IPG)
814 N. Franklin Street,
Chicago, IL 60610, USA
Email: frontdesk@ipgbook.com
Web: http://www.ipgbook.com

China
China Publishers Services Ltd.
718, 7/F., Fortune Commercial Building,
362 Sha Tsui Road, Tsuen Wan, N.T.
Hong Kong
Email: edwin@cps-hk.com

Europe, Oceania, Middle East and Africa
EUROSPAN
1 Bedford Row,
London, WC1R 4BU
United Kingdom
Email: info@eurospan.co.uk
Web: https://www.eurospangroup.com

Southeast Asia
Alkem Company Pte Ltd.
1, Sunview Road #01-27,
Eco-Tech@Sunview
Singapore 627615
Email: enquiry@alkem.com.sg

Japan
MHM Limited
3-2-3F, Kanda-Ogawamachi, Chiyoda-ku,
Tokyo 101-0052
Email: sales@mhmlimited.co.jp
Web: http://www.mhmlimited.co.jp

Library of Congress Control Number: 2024900269

ISBN 978-1-920850-37-1 (hardback)
ISBN 978-1-920850-38-8 (paperback)
ISBN 978-1-920850-39-5 (eBook)

Contents

Figures

Tables

Photographs

Acknowledgements

This book could not have been written without the publication of my previous work, *Panpan to wa dare nano ka?* (Who were *panpan?*). Thanks to the many people who picked it up, I began to communicate with Kazu-san, daughter of Teruyo-san, founder of a long-established ramen restaurant. Kazu-san's storytelling led me unexpectedly to Teruyo-san's rich life story. Beyond my initial intention, *Panpan to wa dare nano ka?* spun out into further encounters with various people, and this book was born. At the same time, I wanted this book to be read by as many people as possible, especially those who had experienced the Occupation, and writing this book proved to be a race against time.

In this publication, I have chosen to withhold the name of Teruyo-san's ramen restaurant. I hope that readers will be able to imagine where this restaurant is located as they read this book. Thank you to Kazu-san and her family for sharing with us many memories of the Occupation that she 'was going to take to [her] grave'.

I would like to thank Mr. Katsuyoshi Tomimoto's son, Mr. Yuji Tomimoto, and his family for his kindness and for allowing me to quote from his memoirs in 'Sengo zeronen' (0 years after the war; broadcast on 15 August 2015 on NHK-BS), as well as Ms. Ayumi Ito, director of NHK Enterprises, who gave me access to Mr. Tomimoto.

I would also like to express my deepest gratitude to the following people: Mr. Taichi Kinugawa, Recercher of Kobe Planet Film Archive, for providing me with many valuable photographs from the Occupation period; Miyoshi Miyazaki, an artist based in Motoko, for locating the photographs of Kobe under the Occupation; Shinichi Tsuji, a supervising researcher of urban and regional planning park management and operation at Environment Green Space Consultants Co. Ltd. who taught me how to create the map; and Shiori Murakami, a researcher of Occupation Kobe, who also allowed me to browse materials related to her research on seized housing in occupied Japan.

In May 2015, I conducted my first interview with Shuhei Yoshinaga of the *Kyoto shimbun* and Kazu-san at a cafe in An-rakuji Temple in Kyoto. The following month, Kazu-san and I met with Mr. Norifumi Nagazumi of the *Kyoto shimbun* to retrace Kazu-san's footsteps during the Occupation period when she was in elementary school. I still remember the taste of the waffle parfait we had at Camphora, a Kyoto University café-restaurant, at the end of our walk on a hot early summer day.

It is a strange coincidence that Kazu's mother, Teruyo, was a senior of Nagasumi and Yoshinaga. Thanks to Ms. Noriko Kitahara, mother of Megumi Kitahara who is professor emeritus of Osaka University, I learned that Teruyo was a reporter for the *Kyoto Nichinichi shimbun*, the predecessor of the *Kyoto shimbun*. Just as this book was nearing completion, Noriko passed away. It is a pity that I could not complete this book while Noriko was still alive.

This book was written using sociological methods to analyze historical materials; it was necessary to properly analyze the vast number of oral histories of sixty-three people as well as Kazu's interviews. I am very grateful to Professor Chizuko Ueno, sociologist and professor emeritus at the University of Tokyo, for her help. I could not have written this book without using Ueno's qualitative method of analysis. At the same time, the members of the Ueno seminar at the Graduate School of Ritsumeikan University, many of whom are working professionals in the field, gave me helpful advice and words of encouragement during the process of writing this book. It is thanks to all of you who welcomed me as peers that I did not fail in the process.

It was Professor Masakazu Tanaka, professor emeritus of Kyoto University, who introduced me to the concept of contact zones. Had I not encountered this theoretical framework, I am not sure whether I would have been able to write this book.

I am grateful to Professor Yuko Nishikawa for her many teachings on Kyoto during the Occupation. Her valuable work, *Koto no Senryo* (The old capital under occupation) was very helpful in completing this book.

This book is based on my essay in *Senso to seiboryoku no hikakushi e mukete* (Toward a comparative history of war and sexual violence), edited by Chizuko Ueno, Shinzo Araragi and Kazuko Hirai (2018), which was published two months earlier than the original Japanese version of this book. I am not sure how much of this book I could have written without the rich discussions I had with my co-authors. I would like to thank all the contributing authors as well as Kumi Ohashi, editor of Iwanami Shoten, for their support.

I received valuable advice from Yachiyo Sudo, professor emeritus of Aichi Prefectural University, one of our co-researchers studying women's poverty in postwar Japan as seen from a women's shelter, based on her experience as a social worker in Kotobukicho, Yokohama over a period of more than thirty years.

I am indebted to Ichiro Tomiyama, our graduate school supervisor, and Emiko Ochiai and Kimio Ito, professor emeritus of Kyoto University. I received valuable information and suggestions from my colleagues in the unit, especially from Ms. Toshiko Tsujimoto at its rotating study group of researchers. I am also grateful to the members of the Murasakino no Kai.

In this publication, I was able to cite a paper by Mr. Hajime Kakita, a friend from my graduate school days, who sadly passed away due to illness.

I would like to thank all my friends for their constant support.

This book is based on my original Japanese book, *Mou-hitotsu no senryo* (Another occupation; Impact Shuppankai, 2018). Only female translators were involved in the translation of this book into English. The Introduction was translated by Dr. Barbara Hartley; Chapter 1 by Dr. Penny Bailey; chapters 2 and 4 and references by Ms. Mariko Kishi-Debski; Chapter 3 by Dr. Helen Kilpatrick; chapters 5 to 7 by Dr. Judy Wakabayashi; Chapter 8 by Dr. Akiko Uchiyama; and the Conclusion by Dr Tomoko Aoyama. I would like to thank all of them.

I would like to thank Ms. Yuko Uematsu, Director of Trans Pacific Press, and her editorial team for their support. This work was supported by Japan Society for the Promotion of Science (KAKENHI) Grant Number 22HP6006.

This book is dedicated to my family, who have always been watching over me at all times.

Toshimi Chazono

Introduction

Occupied Japan after defeat in war: *panpan*, discrimination, stigma

> We didn't call them *panpan* or anything like that. They were our big sisters. They really looked out for us kids on the streets – war orphans, we were. "Sweetie, have you eaten anything today?" Or: "Are you hungry?" they'd ask. And when we said, "No, not yet, we've had nothing today", off they'd go straight away and buy us food.

Katsuyoshi Tomimoto (hereafter Katsuyoshi) was eighty when he gave the interview from which the above excerpt was taken[1]. Katsuyoshi had spent two years living as a war orphan on the streets – a street child in contemporary discourse – after being separated from his family at the age of nine during the Bombing of Tokyo on the night of 9–10 March 1945. When the contingencies of street life and an empty stomach brought him to a complete standstill, it was the women referred to by others as '*panpan*' who reached out to help. The term *panpan* that appears in Katsuyoshi's statement above has long been a pejorative term for women who had sexual relations with Occupation soldiers. Similar labels included *yami no onna*, literally 'women of the dark' although usually translated as 'street prostitute', and *yoru no onna*, 'women of the night'.

In April 2015, a woman called Kazuko Osaka (hereafter Kazu) contacted me after reading a newspaper article about a seminar I convened entitled 'Revisiting sexual violence during the Occupation era'. She wanted to say how kind the women who had sex with Occupation soldiers had been to her when she was in elementary school.

1

I never once heard Kazu use the term '*panpan*'. When I asked why, she replied with a smile:

> [During the Occupation] I realized just how insulting the term *panpan* was. So, I could never say that word. Those women were my big sisters.

Both Kazu and Katsuyoshi gave the same reason for avoiding using the term '*panpan*'. The stigma that marked these women during the Occupation and the contemptuous gaze then directed towards them have continued to the present day. That stigma arose for various reasons. There was, for example, a tendency to regard all women who had sex with Occupation military personnel as prostitutes of one sort or another, while the scornful stare of men in occupied Japan was a sign that they regarded these women as 'sleeping with the enemy'. This contempt is also evident in the anxious terror of the 'protection racket' perpetrated by those such as educator and education critic Kiyoshi Kanzaki, who said of Japanese women having sexual relations with Occupation personnel, 'These are the precious daughters of Japan' (Kanzaki 1974: 202). Sociologist Fumika Sato bluntly defines the 'protection racketeer' as a man who 'promises to protect a woman' (Sato 2018: 334). She goes on to note how men who claim to guard women become frustrated and anxious when they fail and so 'constrain the woman or women targeted' (Sato 2018: 335). In a series of publications, and in contrast to the praise he heaped on Japanese women who refused to marry Occupation personnel, Kanzaki harshly critiqued Japanese women who took the initiative to begin relations with foreign military men (Chazono 2014). We can explain this in terms of the 'protection racketeer' Kanzaki, who failed to 'protect' the women he deemed to be the 'precious daughters of Japan'.

The following discussion considers two social factors that contributed to the stigma attached to women engaging in sexual relations with Occupation forces. The first concerns the opening of 'comfort stations' to cater for these men. Established across Japan, these stations were state facilities providing the 'comfort' of sexual services for both officers and enlisted men. Secondly, neither the women themselves nor those around them were aware that relations ranging from rape through sex work to love and/or marriage between a member of an occupying military and a woman from the country so occupied constituted a continuum of sexual violence. This is because, as sociologist Chizuko Ueno observes, when locating sexual violence on the continuum outlined above, the very fact that the various elements overlap 'makes it difficult to identify the cut-off point between each' (Ueno 2018: 1).

We might return, in this context, to Kazu who declared, 'I thought the story of how my big sisters helped me would go with me to the grave'. Given that no interest whatsoever was shown in her memories of interactions with the women who treated her so kindly, and because those who knew women who had intimate relations with Occupation military told her that they 'didn't know any women like that', it was natural for Kazu to believe that her story would be lost once she passed away. Society has habitually exerted pressure on people such as Kazu and Katsuyoshi to prevent them from talking about their 'good memories' of the women who had intimate relations with Occupation personnel. We have furthermore collectively embargoed the memories of so-called '*panpan*' women themselves. Even those of us who were willing to hear and discuss the precious accounts of these women failed to create a suitable platform for this to occur. Each of these factors has contributed to the social stigmatization of *panpan*.

Photo 0.1 'ANY FOR THE ASKING GEISHA GIRLS IN KOBE'

The agency of women

Photo 0.1 is a privately owned image taken by a member of the Occupation forces in Kobe immediately after the end of World War II.[2] The rubble in the background narrates the situation in Kobe at that time. The caption on the back of the photograph reads, 'Any for the asking geisha girls in Kobe'.

While the date is between 25 September and 1 November 1945, the short sleeves and the summer fabric of the women's attire give the impression that the image was taken in the harsh lingering heat of late September. The women's garb tells us that they are probably hostesses working at a military comfort station in Kobe. Without the rubble we might forget that they belong to a country under occupation. As photos 0.2–0.6 confirm, however, the extreme ravages of war were highly visible in Kobe immediately after the defeat.

At 5.05 pm on 25 September 1945, the Occupation forces arrived in Kobe with a complement of 15,000 personnel from the 6th Army 33rd Infantry Division (Iwasa 1966: 43). As

Photo 0.2 (top-left) 'JAPS CLEANING UP KOBE'
Photo 0.3 (bottom-left) Men removing rubble after World War II
(caption added by the author)
Photo 0.4 (top-right) 'KOBE LOOKING TOWARD THE RAILROAD
STATION PICTURE TAKEN FROM THE BUILDING I LIVED IN'
Photo 0.5 (bottom-right) Kobe where rubble remains after World
War II (caption added by the author)

evident from Photos 0.4 and 0.5, women then largely wore
monpe (women's work pants), although, as seen in Photo 0.6,
women workers dressed in Western trousers that hid the
line of the leg. The contrast in terms of clothing with the five
women in Photo 0.1 is immediately obvious.

Photo 0.1 was taken at a site requisitioned by the occupying military, while the jeep around which the women are
gathered is an Occupation Army jeep. The mountain of rubble
surrounding the vehicle speaks to the impact of defeat in war.
The caption to a different photograph of the same women
reads: 'Corporal Perse who is looking to recruit new geisha
girls'.[3] We might therefore conclude that among these women
there are some who would undoubtedly never have become

Photo 0.6 'X PARKS OUR HOME IN KOBE ONE OF THE FEW BUILDINGS THAT IS STILL STANDING'

'geisha' if there had been no occupation of Japan. Even if they had, in fact, worked as 'geisha' in the past, without Japan's defeat, none would have had contact with occupying military personnel. When analyzing Photo 0.1, we must therefore consider what is hidden behind the smiling faces of these women of a vanquished nation in their gorgeous clothes. We should moreover be aware that there was a dramatic difference in the status of these women compared to the men of their defeated homeland and particularly the male victors.

In these five women and their confident laughter I sense a determination to parry with the Occupation soldier who directs the camera towards them. In other words, we must not overlook the agency that they display. In Chizuko Ueno's definition, this agency is 'actively seeking to exercise one's will even under conditions of constraint' (Ueno 2018: 11).

Aims and themes

The women featured in this book were subjected to the overwhelming violence of occupation. Concrete expressions of such violence were rape by Occupation personnel and being 'rounded-up' (arrested) like stray dogs to be forcibly examined for venereal disease (VD) under the direction of the GHQ (General Headquarters of the Supreme Commander for the Allied Powers) (Chazono 2014). Through profiling the continuum of sexual violence referred to above and further discussed below in terms of rape, sex work, love and marriage committed and engaged in by Occupation personnel, and using the concept of 'contact zone', this book aims to draw attention to what occurred in the space in which Occupation personnel and Japanese women encountered each other.

Women who had sexual relations with Occupation military personnel cannot merely be lumped together and contemptuously dismissed as *panpan*. Rather, these were women who, confronted with the overwhelming imbalance of power that was the Occupation, found a way to survive an era in which they had severely limited options. In the discussion that follows, I will draw on valuable material presented in a 1949 Yuukosya publication, *Gaisho, Jittai to sono Shuki* (Streetwalkers: Reality and personal accounts; hereafter *Streetwalkers*), edited by Katsuo Takenaka and Etsuji Sumiya, to conduct an in-depth inductive analysis and thus detail the survival strategies deployed by these women.

Sociologist Akiko Hashimoto (2017) has discussed Japan's memories of defeat in war from a comparative international perspective. According to Hashimoto, such 'shadow comparison' can 'illuminate patterns in Japan' and thereby 'derive insights into meanings either implicitly or explicitly' (Hashimoto 2015: 20). A 'shadow comparison' method is also effective for the project under discussion here. Given the veto

7

on speaking out imposed on women in Japan who had sexual relations with Occupation military personnel, comparing these women's lives to those of women in Europe who had sexual contact with occupying troops will foreground various elements experienced by both. This is precisely the process referred to by Ueno, Araragi and Hirai (2018: iv) who observe how 'through comparison, the unique aspects of particular examples, in addition to common factors, become apparent for the first time'.

Accordingly, keeping in mind the various ways in which women in areas under German occupation during World War II had sexual contact with German soldiers, the discussion will focus on the agency of Japanese women who had similar relations with armed forces personnel occupying Japan. Attention will also focus on how, in the face of the extraordinary violence of the Occupation itself, these women somehow survived.

In her 2017 Heibonsha monograph entitled *Koto no Senryo* (The old capital under occupation), historian Yuko Nishikawa draws on her own experiences to provide a meticulously detailed account of Kyoto during the Occupation era. Many aspects of the current discussion owe a debt to Nishikawa's text, which seeks to 'guide readers as they walk through the streets of occupied Kyoto' (2017: 374). In this work, I wish to clarify how women, who were sometimes the mothers of mixed-race children, battled to survive. This is the most significant aim of the book and will make a major contribution to positive understandings of Japanese society at the time. In this and previous publications, I have consistently worked on the assumption that what happened to these women was in no way a special set of circumstances unique to the Occupation of Japan. In other words, I do not present their experiences as some sort of special case.

Sources and method of analysis

In addition to the 1949 *Streetwalkers* publication, the discussion in Chapter 4 draws on anecdotes from interviews with Kazu about a woman she was close to during the Occupation era. Chapter 2 also features specific cases of rape documented in GHQ records. Below are details of the various sources used throughout the book.

Streetwalkers: 'personal accounts', 'oral statements' and 'records of stories heard'

Streetwalkers is a survey report of data collected during the GHQ censorship regime from more than 200 women who had had sexual relations with members of the Occupation military in Kyoto's city precincts. The survey was conducted by the Kyoto Social Welfare Research Center (Kyoto Shakai Fukushi Kenkyu jo) under the direction of Emily Putnam, head of the GHQ Military Governance Welfare Section. In November 1949, as noted above, this survey material was published as *Gaisho, Jittai to sono Shuki*.

The Kyoto Social Welfare Research Center was staffed largely by sociologists working in conjunction with medical and administrative staff. From December 1948 to April 1949, the center conducted a fact-finding survey of women who were street-based sex-workers as one of several projects initiated as a matter of urgency at the time. The 'streetwalkers' survey subjects were women who provided remunerated sexual services to members of the Occupation military. Records indicate that Emily Putnam directed staff to conduct all aspects of the project 'in a scientific and objective way'. However, bias is evident in both the results of the survey and in the material produced by individual researchers who analyzed the data. We might therefore question both the nature of the science and whether the final report was, in fact, objective. The very fact that *Streetwalkers'* co-editor and research center head, Katsuo Takenaka, stated that the survey targeted 200 or more women 'streetwalkers' in the Kyoto vicinity (Takenaka and Sumiya, eds., 1949: 6) confirms that it prejudicially assumed this status for each of the women involved. This is notwithstanding, as probed below, how the highly skewed power dynamics that operated under the Occupation resulted in women having various reasons for entering into sexual relations with foreign military personnel. Nevertheless, since eighty-six of the women provided in-depth details about their personal circumstances, the survey interview material is extremely valuable. We must, however, keep in mind that, as Nishikawa importantly observes, 'it is unclear whether the Kyoto Social Welfare Research Center initiated the project independently or whether it was set up with a particular agenda by an individual or group whose identity is unknown' (Nishikawa 2017: 264).

In the book, editors Takenaka and Sumiya explained the survey's data collection method. 'Almost daily', they wrote,

> MPs [US military police] and Japanese police conducted a whole-of-city round-up of "streetwalkers" who were taken to Heian Hospital [the then Kyoto City Venereal Disease Hospital] where they were held for three days to be checked for things such as VDs. We took advantage of those three days to dispatch a staff member to conduct individual interviews. Women in the vicinity of Kyoto Station were rounded up and sent by police or staff for detention at the [Kyoto] Central Protection Center. Editor Etsuji Sumiya himself went there to interview these women. (Takenaka and Sumiya, eds., 1949: 120)

The Kyoto City Central Protection Center was located behind the northern end of the Higashi Honganji Temple precinct. This facility was established immediately after the war by former Kenpeitai (Imperial Army military police) member, Magoharu Sekido, who began providing for homeless people in the vicinity of Kyoto Station. Sekido ran the center with food and other support provided by the Kyoto authorities. Following a series of name changes, the facility became the Kyoto City Central Protection Center in accordance with the 1 October 1946 Public Assistance Law. Although until then residents had largely been homeless people, the facility now also received 'orphans, the elderly and infirm, people with psychiatric conditions, and tuberculosis sufferers, in addition to providing temporary accommodation for "streetwalker" women' (Takenaka and Sumiya, eds., 1949: 290). Women rounded-up in the Kyoto metropolitan area were sent to either Heian Hospital or the protection center and forcibly examined for VDs. Interviews and data collection occurred while women were interned in one of the two facilities discussed above.

Women diagnosed as having a VD were forcibly hospitalized and treated at Heian Hospital until completely clear of infection. If women without infection had a place to which they could return, they were released. Those with no fixed abode were sent to a location known as Shisouen. According to Takenaka and Sumiya, this was a 'social welfare facility' located in Kyoto's Iwakura district where 'streetwalkers were housed in order to re-evaluate their lives with the help of occupational guidance, psychological self-reflection and self-improvement' (Takenaka and Sumiya, eds., 1949: 290). Higashi Honganji Temple was entrusted by the Kyoto authorities with the operation of the facility.

The involvement of Emily Putnam, head of the GHQ Military Governance Welfare Section, suggests that the 200 or more surveys were themselves ultimately presented in report form to GHQ. In addition to that documentation, material assembled by Yoshiichi Kogamo, the administrative superintendent of the Kyoto City Central Protection Center, constitutes a valuable source that has facilitated the survey analysis conducted in this book. Kogamo's job included administrative tasks such as interviewing and counselling the homeless, compiling various reports on work surveys, providing lifestyle and work advice to facility residents and producing medical treatment coupons. Takenaka writes in the *Streetwalkers* foreword, 'the personal accounts compiled by Yoshiichi Kogamo are particularly hard to come by', seeming to confirm that the personal accounts and other materials appearing in *Streetwalkers* were in fact prepared by the Kyoto Social Welfare Research Center.

The introductory section to the 'Personal accounts of streetwalkers' part of the book explains, 'All style matters including sentence structure, wording and the use of kana have been retained with no corrections. Some are extremely difficult to decipher'. This suggests that research center staff did their best to ensure that no changes were made to the original form of the personal accounts provided by the women interviewed. Strictly speaking, however, it is difficult now to determine the extent to which the women's words were modified and it is likely that some degree of editorial intervention occurred. Moreover, since *Streetwalkers* was published under the Occupation censorship regime, there are small redactions here and there making it difficult to say with honesty that 'all style matters have been retained'.

Notwithstanding these issues, the availability of these women's personal accounts allows an in-depth analysis of their stories and of the sexual contact between members of the Occupation military personnel and Japanese women. The discussion moreover seeks to re-confirm that having sex with Occupation military personnel during the confusion created by the deep wounds left by Japan's defeat was one of only a few survival choices available to women.

The editors of the *Streetwalkers* materials explained the data collection process as follows:

> The survey itself was conducted by the research center from December 1948 to April 1949, with individual interviews of more than 200 women. Interviewers took the time to use in-depth questioning techniques that enabled them to ascertain the women's actual circumstances, including their personal feelings or emotional state. Staff involved also collected a significant volume of written and oral accounts, letters and memos, in addition to making notes concerning the stories they heard. It is this meticulous attention to detail that undoubtedly gives special value to the research center surveys. (Takenaka and Sumiya, eds., 1949: 121)

Eighty-six respondents provided particularly valuable information. These comprised fifteen 'streetwalker personal accounts' and sixty 'streetwalker oral statements' (among these narratives, five were unnumbered while the list also had many missing numbers). Eleven were 'records of stories told by streetwalkers'; that is, they were second-hand accounts compiled by interviewers. All others, nonetheless, can be regarded as the 'living voices' of the women concerned. It was initially assumed that the inclusion of second-hand 'records of stories' occurred because the interviewees were unable to write. It is apparent, however, that among this group were women who had received a prewar higher education. In other words, there should have been no need for interviewers to take notes instead of the women writing the information themselves. Since no other details are available, however, the exact reason for this category remains unclear.

While narratives in the collection are numbered consecutively, there are various anecdotes that remain unnumbered. *Streetwalkers* is silent on the contents of the skipped numbers and the related narratives. This is particularly the case among the second-hand 'records of the personal accounts of streetwalkers', which often abruptly commence with a number although many numbers are skipped. Nishikawa noted how, at an Occupation era research seminar, it was suggested that 'entries with skipped or missing numbers might refer not to ordinary enlisted men but to personnel of sergeant rank or higher who were the regular partners of women and that cards with this information might have been concealed or disposed of' (Nishikawa 2017: 255). While this explanation is completely plausible, there are two further possibilities. First, a rounded-up woman may have been having sex, not with an officer, but with one of the non-commissioned rank MPs who carried out the actual raid. Second, she may have been the legal wife of an Occupation solider. It is likely that in these or similar instances numbers would be missing.

The ages of the contributing women ranged from sixteen to thirty-six, with an average of twenty-one. The majority, furthermore, had been educated to secondary level (including those who did not complete this level of schooling) or higher.

Ministry of Education Survey Bureau figures that give the female student retention rate from elementary to secondary education as 16.5 percent in 1935 and twenty-two percent in 1940 (Ministry of Education Survey Bureau, ed., 1962: 39) confirm that, prior to Occupation era system reforms, only girls from well-off families were able to advance in that way (Uchida, ed., and Yayoi Art Museum 2005). It is therefore apparent that it was women of relatively high social standing who had intimate relationships with Occupation military personnel.

Of the eighty-six women referred to above, twenty-three were in relationships with Japanese men. These are excluded to allow the discussion to focus on the sixty-three who had sexual relationships with members of the Occupation military. Recorded with the narrative of each woman was a current address (or place of birth, or both current address and place of birth), date of birth and, according to the records, a pseudonym. Nevertheless, because today it is impossible to determine the extent to which pseudonyms were, in fact, used, and in order not to reveal specific information about the women, this book gives each either the name of a flower or a seasonal name associated with a flower. This decision does not relate to the fact that those discussed are women and does not reflect the symbolic association between flowers and femininity. Following a traffic accident, I lost my sense of smell for ten years during which time I was unable to recognize floral fragrances or the seasonal changes these announced. I was also unable to recall the pleasant memories inextricably evoked by those fragrances. I accordingly chose floral pseudonyms for the women whose stories appear in this discussion in the hope that overlapping their lives with my own experience might permit me to reveal as far as possible the feelings of women denied the chance to voice their memories in public until now.

GHQ documents concerning rape in occupied Japan

In addition to the materials discussed above, I consulted GHQ documentation related to rape. The 'Weekly Summary of Events' produced by the GHQ's Criminal Investigation Division (CID) provided a schedule on a week-by-week basis of incidents involving Allied military personnel in occupied Japan.[4] These incidents included cases of the rape of Japanese women by members of the occupying forces.

Press Code regime that operated in occupied Japan made it impossible for the press to discuss cases of rape perpetrated by occupying military. Hiroshi Harada, a member of the Japanese police who was popularly known as 'The MP Rider' who acted as a translator in the company of US Armed Forces MPs during Occupation city jeep patrols, observed as follows:

> Even when American troops committed robbery, nothing appeared in press articles. A writer could merely say something general like: "The offender was tall with black skin". To write that an American soldier committed a crime was a violation of the Occupation Press Code. There were many occasions, therefore, when news reporters rushed to the scene of a major traffic accident only to give up taking notes and quickly return home when they realized that members of the American military were involved. (Harada 1994: 97)

While the documentation related to rape referenced in this study was circulated internally within Occupation ranks, it was never made public in newspaper reports. The objective of the book is to draw attention to the rapes of women committed in occupied Japan during the period around 1949, and to consider both the form these rapes took and the survival strategies adopted by the women who were assaulted. Ultimately, by reading GHQ reports related to the rape of women in occupied Japan, documentation produced by the very entity to which those who committed the rapes were attached, and juxtaposing these with the anecdotal records of personal accounts by the women 'streetwalkers' themselves who were subjected to these rapes, I will emphatically confirm the overwhelming power imbalance imposed on women in occupied Japan.

Stories by the living witness, Kazu

The book draws upon new and important documentation not referenced in previous works. This is the oral record of Kazu who, during the Occupation, received support and kindness from women who were involved in sexual relationships with members of the occupying military. Using a digital voice recorder, I interviewed Kazu on various occasions between May 2015 and December 2016 during which she spoke freely about her experiences of the time. This raw data was analyzed using the 'Ueno method' (see Ueno, Ichinomiya and Chazono, eds., 2017).

Structure of the book

Chapter 1 details the context of the social system that gave rise to the stigma associated with the expression '*panpan*'. Chapters 2 to 5 foreground the themes of rape and sex work, in addition to love and marriage, while conducting a thematic investigation of the concrete individual survival strategies of Japanese women involved in intimate relationships with members of the occupying armed forces. Chapter 6 will provide examples of cases of rape/prostitution/love/marriage that existed on the continuum from pressured involvement to coercion by force (Kelly 2001: 96–97). Focusing on cases of marriage to an Occupation soldier and the birth of mixed-race children, Chapter 7 will consider examples from Germany and France as a means of identifying the conditions necessary for Japan's silenced women and children to voice their own experiences.

Every attempt has been made to dispense with the use of specialist language and to confine commentary and annotations to a minimum. Since there will be readers who are unfamiliar with Occupation era circumstances, language used in quotes and citations has, as necessary, been modified to contemporary Japanese. Furthermore, while in the original documentation ages recorded at the time of the survey are given in the old Japanese age system (one year old at birth, with a year added the following New Year's Day), in the discussion that follows these ages are given in Western style. *Fuseji* – symbols such as crosses in a text indicating censored words or passages – have been retained in citations and extracts, while additional explanatory material is contextualized, as appropriate, to accord with nomenclature such as Occupation Army, MP, Occupation military personnel, officer, or Occupation soldier. In spite of gender issues now associated with the term, I use the word 'nurse' (*kangofu*) as was the practice at the time. Explanations added to citations by myself as author are indicated by the use of square brackets ([...]).

Chapter 1

The Institutional Context From Which the Stigma of *Panpan* Emerged

The concept of the 'contact zone'

The investigations in this book have been carried out with two works in mind: Mary L. Roberts's *What Soldiers Do: Sex and the American GI in World War II France* (2013) and Regina Mühlhäuser's *Sex and the Nazi Soldier: Violent, Commercial and Consensual Encounters During the War in the Soviet Union, 1941–45* (2020, translated by Jessica Spengler). These works both analyze the diversity of sexual contacts between soldiers and local women in Europe during World War II. More specifically, *What Soldiers Do* examines how, as the liberators of France, the US military dealt with the sexual activities of their soldiers, while *Sex and the Nazi Soldier* addresses the diverse sexual encounters between the occupying German soldiers and the women of the occupied territories.

For Japanese nationals, the US Army was an occupying force rather than a liberating force as it was for the French nationals in *What Soldiers Do*. The sexual relations between occupying German soldiers and French women in the occupied territories discussed in *Sex and the Nazi Soldier* do bear some similarities with the situation in occupied Japan. However, my book focuses on the postwar period following Japan's defeat, when the Occupation soldiers were not engaged in combat. In addition, while the European works concentrate on the sexual behaviors of the soldiers, the focus of this volume is on the women who entertained the soldiers.

This book takes up the voices of Japanese women who were stigmatized as *'panpan'* and subjected to the public's contemptuous gaze or consumption in the spaces of occupied Japan, where violence resulting from the overwhelming asymmetry (or inequality) of power was rampant. In re-examining their narratives through the concept of the 'contact zone', the study elucidates aspects of the survival strategies they employed within the personal and material limitations of their circumstances.

Here we will pause briefly to discuss the contact zone, a key concept for understanding the behavior of the women in occupied Japan who were in sexual contact with the Occupation soldiers. The contact zone is a concept proposed by the literary scholar Mary L. Pratt:

> The term "contact" foregrounds the interactive, improvisational dimensions of imperial encounters so easily ignored or suppressed by accounts of conquest and domination told from the invader's perspective. A "contact" perspective emphasizes how subjects get constituted in and by their relations to each other. It treats the relations among colonizers and colonized, or travelers and "travelees," not in terms of separateness, but in terms of co-presence, interaction, interlocking understandings and practices, and often within radically asymmetrical relations of power. (Pratt 2007 [1992]: 8)

Thus, the conceptual framework of the contact zone emphasizes the effects of the interactions between the powerful and the powerless, rather than focusing on the conflict between them in relationships marked by asymmetrical power.

This book applies this concept through an examination of that space in occupied Japan where the Occupation soldiers from the victorious side and the Japanese women from the defeated side meet and engage in mutual negotiation.[1] Looking at the relationship between the soldiers and the women from the vantage point of the contact zone, we realize that despite being exposed to the overwhelming violence of the Occupation, the women were able to negotiate with the soldiers and take control of their circumstances by exercising their own agency. As we will see in more detail later, the contact zone is also a concept that has powerful implications for women's resistance to rape.

Additionally, the notion of limited survival strategies is another important concept closely related to the contact zone. Ueno has argued that no one can deny that among the survival strategies of the former 'comfort women' (*ianfu*) of the Imperial Japanese Army there existed a 'voluntary relationship' that the parties called 'love' or 'romance'. Acknowledging that 'voluntary' aspect to the relationships does not in any way negate the oppressive circumstances in which the women found themselves (Ueno 2017b: 252). A striking example of this is the 'love' of a former comfort woman of the Japanese military, Ok-ju Mun, who died in the midst of a military postal savings lawsuit (Mun 1996). The battlefield where Mun found herself in the role of a Korean 'comfort woman' was a place of overwhelmingly asymmetrical violence. One of the survival strategies Mun employed in order to withstand her circumstances was to fall in love with 'Ichiro Yamada', whom she befriended at a military brothel. Mun found her reason for living in Ichiro Yamada's weekly visits. In spite of this, the more she talked of her love for Yamada, the more she demonstrated her pro-Japanese agency, thus making it more difficult in the public sphere for her to be recognized as a victim because her story is distanced from the narratives of victims who actively resisted the Japanese soldiers. Importantly, historian Mikiyo Kano has extrapolated from Mun's case that 'no matter how harsh the situation, people can freely use survival strategies to search out their identities and even nurture love' (2017: 199). It cannot be overemphasized that this notion of 'voluntary relationships' performed by the former comfort women of the Japanese Army also applies to the Japanese women who had intimate relationships with Occupation military personnel.

In the overwhelmingly asymmetrical relationship of the occupying and the occupied, the contact zone is the space in which the women of occupied Japan exercise their own agency to mutually negotiate with the Occupation soldiers; the 'voluntary relationships' between these women and the soldiers in this space is one of a limited number of survival strategies that they can draw on in order to endure the Occupation. Nevertheless, as Sato points out, 'it is not the subject of the narrative that is the problem, it is the prescriptive power of the master narrative of war in a society that ascribes legitimacy to certain narratives – whether they belong to victims or perpetrators – and refuses to listen to those that deviate from them' (2018: 333). If society deems that these women are in a 'consensual relationship' with the enemy occupiers of Japan, their limited survival strategies become obscured. As a result, if the women suffer sexual violence, it is regarded as a consequence of 'self-responsibility'. Seventy years after the end of the Occupation, it is still the case that these women have not received due recognition.

Accordingly, taking up the overwhelmingly asymmetrical relationship of the occupier/occupied, this volume conceptualizes the contact zone as a space in which the women under occupation exercised their own agency to mutually negotiate with the Occupation soldiers, and analyses the 'voluntary relationships' between the women and the soldiers as one of a limited number of survival strategies that they were able to use to endure the period of occupation.

The context of the system

The establishment of comfort facilities and the women selected as 'bulwarks': the case of Kobe city

One reason for the creation of the neologism '*panpan*' and its subsequent stigmatization is deeply embedded in the establishment of 'comfort facilities' for the Occupation forces. On 18 August 1945, the Ministry of Home Affairs implemented an emergency directive to 'hasten the construction of comfort facilities for the occupying forces' so that they would be ready in time for their arrival. Soon after, such facilities were established across Japan.

The establishment of these comfort facilities was fraught with contradictions. The editorial director of the *Hyogo shimbun* (Hyogo Newspaper, an affiliate of the *Kobe shimbun* [Kobe Newspaper]), Jun Iwasa, recorded his feelings at that time:

> Ordinary virtuous women and girls must be protected from the wolf-like qualities of the occupying forces. The [Hyogo] Prefectural Police Headquarters, under central direction, rushed to set up comfort facilities as a bulwark. [The idea was to] save the majority of women by sacrificing the professional and semi-professional women. It was a distressing justification. The plan was to build rooms for prostitutes who would service the US military that the police would keep an eye on. The whole situation made me feel mortified and miserable. All for the sake of protecting the girls of respectable families. (Iwasa 1966: 41)

Twenty years after the end of the war, Iwasa compiled the articles he had written for the newspaper in 'Rimenshi, himerareta shinso' (Hidden histories and hidden truths) as part of *Hyogo: Fusetsu nijunen* (Hyogo: A twenty-year ordeal) published by the Hyogo Newspaper Company in 1966. As the opening pages of the work contain manuscripts by key members of the political and financial sphere, old and new, who were responsible for the administration and finances of Hyogo prefecture and Kobe city – including Motohiko Kanai (governor of Hyogo prefecture), Chujiro Haraguchi (mayor of Kobe), Chohei Asada (member of the Kobe Chamber of Commerce and Industry), Yukio Kishida (former governor of Hyogo prefecture and member of the House of Councillors), and Kazuo Nakai (former mayor of Kobe) – we can assume that these figures acknowledged the content of the narratives concerning the establishment of comfort facilities for the occupying forces.

From Iwasa's words, it is possible to ascertain that when the comfort facilities for the dedicated use of the Occupation forces opened across Japan, women had already been classified into groups of those who were to be sacrificed for the state, and those who were not. Although the circumstances surrounding the installation and naming of the facilities differed according to region (Hayakawa 2007; Hirai 2014),[2] one thing they all had in common was that it was decided that 'professional and semi-professional women' (Iwasa 1966: 41) would be the first to be presented to the occupying forces as 'sexual bulwarks'.

The idea of a dedicated comfort facility for the occupying forces, a state project initiated under the pretext of creating a 'sexual bulwark', is reminiscent of the sexual comfort stations of the Japanese military in Korea as well as the 'bulwark' of rape by Soviet soldiers against repatriates from Manchuria. A common characteristic among these three cases is that those women who were not deemed 'ordinary women and girls' were the first to be offered up as sexual bulwarks. In Manchuria, 'women engaged in sexual services' (Furukubo 1999: 5) and so-called 'women in special occupations' (Yamamoto 2013: 31) were distinguished from 'ordinary women'.[3]

Interestingly, Mühlhäuser's research into the military prostitution establishments built by Hitler's national security forces (hereafter, referred to as the Wehrmacht) in various places in the occupied territories during World War II brought to light that there is nothing in the archives to indicate any objective criteria behind their creation. She makes the fascinating point that the revelation of homosexual contact among soldiers was one of the reasons for the establishment of prostitution facilities (2020: 154). After analyzing a number of documents discussing homosexuality within the Wehrmacht, Mühlhäuser quotes Thomas Kühne, who states that 'the lines between tender, comforting comradeship and homosexuality were sometimes blurry' (Mühlhäuser 2020: 185, note 236). Naturally, the Wehrmacht may have had reason to set up a 'sexual bulwark' to prevent 'savage' behaviors, but the idea that the Japanese established prostitution facilities in order to prevent homosexual contact in the military is yet to be clarified, both in the case of the Japanese military comfort stations and in the case of the Occupation military comfort facilities that were installed by the Japanese state not long after the defeat. However, Yasuhiro Okada, who has analyzed the African American troops stationed in Gifu prefecture in occupied Japan through interviews with those soldiers, as well as primary source documents held by the US National Archives and Records Administration, makes the astute point that 'homosexuals and homosexual behaviors were tolerated in black troops stationed in occupied Japan due to the prevalence of venereal diseases and the racial prejudices of white commanders' (2011: 89). Okada's point is limited to the 24th Infantry Regiment at Camp Gifu, but based on his interviews with the soldiers, he was able to ascertain that the background to the relatively tolerant atmosphere towards homosexuality was because 'the spread of venereal diseases through heterosexual sexual activity was becoming a serious problem' and that 'rather than cracking down on the homosexuals in the group, the spread of disease was considered a more serious concern because it was a cause of low morale and a loss of military vigor'. Additionally, it was thought that 'Commander Halloran's racial prejudice against black soldiers led to attitudes that could be seen as an acceptance of, or perhaps even indifference towards, gay black soldiers, including officers' (2011: 88). Okada's analysis suggests that, in opposition to the Germans, who set up prostitution facilities to prevent homosexual contact in the military, homosexuality amongst occupying African American troops in Japan was tolerated in order to prevent the spread of venereal diseases (VDs). It should be noted, however, that the acceptance of homosexuality during the Occupation was rooted in racial prejudice against African American soldiers.

The 'comfort women' issue is not only a 'crime of the state' but also a 'sexual crime committed by men' (Ueno [1998] 2012). This perspective of a dual state/male crime in the establishment of the comfort facilities for the Occupation forces cannot be disregarded, as it was the men from various organizations and the authorities who 'offered up' the women for their services.

In addition to the prostitution facilities set up for the Wehrmacht, there were also prostitution facilities established for forced laborers in Germany. According to historian Toshiko Himeoka, the latter facilities were created in ten concentration camps (starting with Mauthausen in 1942 and including Auschwitz in early 1945) as a means of encouraging camp laborers to increase their workplace production efficiency. However, access to the prostitution facilities was limited to a few privileged prisoners, such as those who held certain positions among the prison population or held special jobs, and Jews were not eligible (Himeoka 2018: 231–32). Among the privileged prisoners, there were no women, and no Jews. That is, in this case, prostitution facilities were set up in concentration camps for privileged male prisoners, while women were forced into sex work by the men who were the leaders of those camps.

In the case of Japan, Nishikawa's research confirms that after the war, the cabaret proprietors who worked closely with the Japanese military and set up entertainment facilities for the troops in mainland China opened comfort facilities for the occupying forces at the request of the government. As Nishikawa points out, 'colonial expansion, the war, the defeat and the Occupation, as well as the postwar period were continuous in terms of people, commodities and structures, without any ruptures' (2017: 245). Similarly, the 'sexual bulwark' of women during the Occupation needs to be viewed from the perspective of continuity in the wartime period.

The Hyogo Prefectural Police Safety Division was abolished in February 1944, but was then subsequently re-established on 22 August 1945 to carry out emergency orders issued by the Ministry of Home Affairs (Hyogo Prefectural Police History Compilation Committee 1975). The liaison officer of the safety division became the clerk for the comfort facilities, and went to great effort to ensure that the comfort facilities for the occupying forces ran smoothly. In the case of Kobe city, it was thought that 1,000 women would be required, but at the end of the war, only 150 prostitutes continued to operate across barely twenty establishments in the Futabashinchi and Maruyama areas of Nagata ward. The immense shortfall in numbers led to the recruitment of women other than those who were 'professional and semi-professional' (Iwasa 1966: 41). Using newspaper employment advertising and notices pasted on telephone poles and other places near train stations, an urgent recruitment drive was organized, ostensibly seeking women 'dancers' and 'hostesses'.

In Germany, it was the Schutzstaffel (SS) who managed the prostitution facilities for forced laborers.[4] The SS initially attempted to secure sex workers for these facilities through voluntary applications from women detained on the basis of 'prostitution'. However, because they received only a small amount of interest, in the end most of the women involved were semi-forcibly selected as sex workers (Himeoka 2018: 232). The initial act of attempting to make women entangled in 'prostitution' perform sex work in prostitution facilities for forced laborers is on par with the gathering of service women for the establishment of comfort facilities for the Occupation forces by the Hyogo Prefectural Police Safety Division mentioned earlier. In both cases, the fact that women with a history of 'prostitution' would work as sex workers was seen as axiomatic.

The method for recruiting sex workers for the German prostitution facilities was first based on the selection of 100 good-looking women. After they had showered, the SS inspected their naked bodies, and selected fifty women with no signs of ulcers or rashes (Himeoka 2018: 232). Quoting an article by Schultz (1994), Himeoka relays how the SS 'enjoyed their selections, describing their vulgar and derisive impressions' (Himeoka 2018: 232). Since the selection of women forced into sex work by the men in these organizations was itself a form of sexual violence, the

Photo 1.1 'BUILDING OF LOVE'

establishment of concentration camp comfort facilities in Germany can be thought of as multi-layered 'sexual crimes carried out by men'.[5]

The caption of Photo 1.1 is 'Building of Love'.[6] Inside the oval outline (added by the author) there are many beds lined up in rows in the front of the building, which is under renovation. The fact that the beds outnumber the building's window frames indicates that the structure is a dedicated comfort facility for the Occupation forces. For the photographer – an Occupation soldier – the building under renovation with its many beds represents an exotic oasis where he can forget about the battlefield and serves as a symbol of nurturing 'love' with the women of the conquered country. It is for this reason that the photograph was given its caption.

However, would the hostesses who provided sexual company for the soldiers in this facility have considered it a 'building of love'? Without the Occupation, there would have been no dedicated comfort facilities and no hostesses for the occupying troops. The way this photo is captioned indicates the violence of the Occupation's overwhelming power asymmetry.

On 20 February 1948, the *Kobe shimbun* published an interesting account of a roundtable discussion between intellectuals and a number of *machi no onna* (street women; a synonym for *panpan*) titled 'A talk with street women'. One of the women who participated in the discussion reveals that her younger sister was a hostess at a comfort facility for the occupying forces. She explains that her sister's motivation for applying for the job was that 'initially she was invited to apply under attractive names such as "special dancer" and was offered special rice rations'. This implies that there was recruitment of sex workers on the pretext that they would work as 'special dancers'.[7]

The following is a description of the *ianfu* (comfort women) at the dedicated comfort facility for the occupying forces in Kobe:

> Anyway, the *ianfu* were all organized. At the same time, the comfort facilities that would house these women and welcome the American soldiers were constructed at a rapid pace. The rice and kimonos had to be sourced for the women who agreed to work there on that promise. It was an era of low supplies, and special priority rationing procedures had been put in place. Negotiations had to be made about the vacating of buildings, and flush toilets, beds and bedding supplies all had to be arranged. (Iwasa 1966: 42)

The 'special rice rations' mentioned above refers to the rice that was distributed with special preference. This was an era when even substitute foods for rice gruel, such as potatoes and soy beans, were in short supply. Sacrifices had to be made in order to solve more pressing problems. As a result, even the daughters of respectable families with no experience applied (Iwasa 1966: 42).

In circumstances where commodities were scarce and there was a lack of shelter due to the war, and families were dispersed or trying to avoid becoming destitute, it must have been difficult to resist the 'charm' of 'being able to wear a beautiful kimono and eat lots of food', no matter how much the women were said to be 'volunteering with free will'.[8] Here, again, the line between volunteering and coercion is difficult to draw.

The dresses and fine clothes worn by the five women in the introduction to this volume (Photo 0.1) were only made possible because the establishment of the comfort facilities for the occupying forces was a state project. Furthermore, according to *Black Glasses Like Clark Kent* (Svoboda 2011), written by Terese Svoboda, a niece of Don Svoboda who was stationed as an MP in occupied Japan, brothels during the Occupation were called 'geisha houses' by the Occupation soldiers. In the statement 'The true geishas before the war never engaged in prostitution' in the *Soldiers Guide to Japan*, the authors inadvertently revealed that misinformation had spread to the US about 'geisha' being a generic term for 'prostitute'.

> The dedicated comfort facilities for the occupying forces were very busy with the soldiers. 'Operation Comfort Station' was also a success. The US soldiers queued up wearing their uniforms, their bayonets still at their sides. White soldiers, black soldiers, and commissioned officers alike were hungry for women. The police were heartened to see that each patiently waited his turn in line. The employees (the comfort women) at the comfort facility were

frightened at first, but gradually they began to smile again. Unlike Japanese men, they were surprisingly well-mannered and gentle. […] Anyway, rough treatment of the ordinary women and girls was avoided. It was a hidden achievement of the sad victims. (Iwasa 1966: 43–44)

Iwasa's quotation ends with the sentence 'At the same time, the prefectural and municipal officials were also worried about the women's care of high-ranking officers'. It does not mention how this was reconciled, but what is noteworthy about this comment is that it indicates that the general appeal published in Kobe city newspapers to recruit service women for comfort facilities was targeted at servicing Occupation soldiers who were not high-ranking officers, and that there were distinctions established according to rank.

Additionally, Iwasa's reference to the 'hidden achievement of the sad victims' refers to the women of occupied Japan who were offered as hostesses at such facilities. It was, after all, the men holding positions of authority who offered them up for their services.

The emergence of '*panpan*' due to Occupation policy: the transition from bulwarks to criminals

The appearance of the *panpan* was not spontaneous, but the result of Occupation policy. A comfort facility for the use of Occupation soldiers was opened on 26 September 1945; on 15 December that year, General Headquarters (GHQ) declared a ban on Occupation soldiers entering that facility. As a result, less than three months after it opened, the facility was closed down due to the spread of VDs among the soldiers who frequented it. In the case of Hyogo prefecture, the ban was a precursor to the abolition of the public prostitution system in Japan announced by GHQ on 22 January 1946. Records indicate that 'more than 1,000 comfort women lost their jobs and gradually became street prostitutes – the so-called *panpan* girls' (Hyogo Prefectural Police History Compilation Committee, ed., 1975: 515). That is, the hostesses who became unemployed soon after new year became prostitutes.

On 20 December 1945, the *Kobe shimbun* reported on arrests made three days after the closure of the comfort facility for occupying forces in Kobe. This was the first time the term *yami no onna* (women of the dark) appeared in the press. The newspaper headline read 'Voluntary corps members end up women of the dark – daughters of elite families among those caught in controlled network'. Bearing in mind that many of the women who were rounded up had served in the service volunteer corps during the war, the following words of Crawford F. Sams, Director of Public Health and Welfare at GHQ, point again to the gravity of the social context:

> During the war, thousands of young women had been brought into the cities from rural areas to work in the war and other industries. They had been housed in dormitories. At the last stage of the war with the tremendous destruction that had occurred, many of these industries had been destroyed. All war industry production was suspended by direction of the occupation. Many of these girls had lost their families— their families having been killed or dispersed as a result of the bombing attacks on the cities. Because many of them had been school girls before being brought to work in the war industries, they knew no other occupation. There being no longer any war industry, they then turned to prostitution as a means of earning a living. There was, therefore, a major social and economic problem involved in the control of venereal disease in Japan. (Sams 1998: 106)

Considering that the military comfort facilities for Occupation forces were part of the state project, like the munitions factories during the war, those women who were conscripted to the munitions industry and then worked as hostesses in the comfort facilities after the war consequently 'served' the state continuously both during and after the war. In spite of this, with the sudden closure of the Occupation's dedicated comfort facilities, they were targeted as 'criminals' who were caught spreading VDs. Furthermore, what these women were forced to accept as an alternative to a 'redundancy payment' was stigmatization as *panpan*. Because the stigma concerned sexual matters, it was difficult for the stigmatized party to make their plight public.

The *Kobe shimbun* did not report anything about the hostesses who worked at the comfort facilities for the occupying forces. Considering that the women were unable to report their circumstances to the press due to GHQ's regulations on free speech at the time, it seems likely that among those arrested there would have been some who had been hostesses at the comfort facilities. Furthermore, in light of the fact that the arrests were conducted three days after the closure of the facility, it would not be surprising to learn that the closure was decided on well before the actual closure date, and that a plan to carry out the arrests three days later was discussed between GHQ and senior police management at the time. There are indications that the authorities had expected in advance that the women who had worked as hostesses in the comfort facilities and suddenly lost their jobs would tout for soldiers on the streets (so-called streetwalkers). The street arrests were not precisely planned. In an interview during the Occupation, Nishikawa learned that 'a restaurant owner's daughters, who had grown up in Kobe and dressed in fashionable clothing, were walking along

Shijo dori together when suddenly the younger one was forced into the sidecar of an Occupation forces motorbike that stopped in front of them, and taken to the Odate building where the headquarters were located'. She was taken away 'because of her nylon socks' (Nishikawa 2017: 148).

In a similar arrest in broad daylight in Beppu city, Oita prefecture, on 1 February 1949, a GHQ report states that a woman who had gone to pick up some rations with her mother was bundled away while waiting for her mother, who was inside the building. The Beppu incident was reported by the Oita prefectural government to GHQ's Oita Prefectural Military Administration.[9] The woman immediately tried to let her mother know, but her captors refused, roughly pushing her into a jeep and taking her to a police station (Chazono 2014: 195). In this case, the report does not state what the deciding factor in the arrest was (Goodrich 1949),[10] but it is clear from the Kyoto case that the MP had criteria for immediate arrest even for trivial matters such as wearing nylon socks.

In the case of Kobe, the authorities needed to prevent false arrests as much as possible, as they were in the initial phase of the apprehension process. For this reason, it is not surprising that they targeted the women who worked as hostesses at the recently closed comfort facilities. The security bureau, which worked with the MP to make arrests, was in charge of the women; in other words, it was the organization that managed their bodies, and therefore knew them very well. Rather than risk damage to the public reputation of the authorities or cause any impediments to future arrests by making false ones, it was convenient for the authorities to target the former hostesses of the comfort facilities.

As we have seen, the 'emergence of Japan's *panpan* girls' did not occur in a vacuum. To begin with, the very idea of procuring hostesses to work in the comfort facilities was based on discrimination against prostitutes. Moreover, the facilities were designed to provide sexual comfort for men from the victorious countries occupying Japan, prepared by the men who worked for those in power. The hostesses who offered sexual comfort to the men on the victorious side in those facilities were recruited by men working for Japanese organizations. Nevertheless, in addition to being discriminated against as 'prostitutes', these women were stigmatized as 'women who had turned to the men on the victorious side' and were thus subjected to the contemptuous gaze of the public.

Reinforcing stigmatization through claims of 'model victims' of false arrests

One of the reasons that the stigmatization of *panpan* was further reinforced was the repeated false arrests on the part of the authorities. Here, a 'false arrest' refers to being apprehended and forced to undergo VD screening despite not being infected with a VD.

The reason why the complaints of the women who were falsely arrested attracted media attention and were taken up at the National Diet (Chazono 2014: 188–189) was because they were 'model victims'. A 'model victim' in this sense is one who can claim that she was 'unfairly arrested despite not being a *panpan*'.

In one case, it was reported that two women were falsely arrested on 15 November 1946. In response, two Socialist Party members of parliament, Shizue Kato and Hisako Yoneyama, visited the Metropolitan Police Department to protest the attitude of the authorities, who they claimed had treated the detained women like 'women of the dark' (*Asahi shimbun*, 7

Table 1.1 Summary of false arrests reported in newspapers

Date	Time	Area	Profession	What the women were doing
15 Nov. 1946	19:30	Ikebukuro	Two film company employees	On the way back home
31 May 1947	19:30	Nagoya	Unknown	Chatting with a friend near her home
4 May 1948	20:00	Yurakucho	Two nurses working at St Luke's Hospital	On the way back home
			English teacher at a church	

December 1946). In another case in Nagoya, a woman who was falsely arrested committed suicide by poisoning herself in hospital. The captions of the 31 May 1947 edition of the *Asahi shimbun*, which reported the case in considerable detail, read: 'Suspected of being a "street woman", "purity" answered with death: Woman's truth earnestly recorded in notebook'; 'Maiden protests with death: Prove my chastity with an autopsy'; and 'Outrage at being treated as a woman of the dark'. In yet another case on 4 May 1948, three women each fell victim to false arrest on their way home from work (*Fujin Minshu shimbun* [Women's democratic newspaper], 4 May 1948). The beginning of this article states as follows:

> The unfair labor problems of the Nichi'eiren [Japanese Motion Picture and Theatrical Workers' Union] and other workplaces that employ women, have recently treated serious working women as "women of the dark", subjecting them to forced medical examinations and unbearable suffering, arousing the indignation of all women and finally leading to the formation of the *Josei o mamoru kai* [Women's Protection Society]. However, just as it seemed that the

growing resentment of all women changed the authorities'
attitudes a little, the same issue appeared once more within
the jurisdiction of Chiyoda ward in Tokyo.

The common denominator among these articles is that each
rails against cases where women have been mistakenly
arrested as 'women of the dark', the so-called *panpan*. The
formation of the Women's Protection Society in 1946 was a
manifestation of the anger over the false arrests of women
working in film and the arrest process itself; it did not proffer
criticism about the violence prostitutes suffered on a daily
basis, and there was no talk of solidarity with them (Ohara,
Shiobara and Ando 1972: 189; Fujime 1997: 328). Even the *Fujin
Minshu shimbun* (Women's democratic newspaper), which
was launched in August 1946 and 'edited entirely by women'
(Sata 1983), did not include *panpan* amongst 'all women'.
One of the members of the Women's Democratic Club (Fujin
Minshu Club), the newspaper's parent organization, was
Shizue Kato, the Socialist Party member who went to the
Metropolitan Police Department to protest against the false
arrest of the two film company employees.

The six women who featured in the print media cited
above either had special social connections or came from
elite backgrounds. The connections of the two women working for the film company were such that when they contacted
the women's section of the company's trade union, two
members of the Socialist Party immediately sought out the
relevant authorities in protest. Two of the remaining four
were nurses working at St Luke's Hospital (present-day
St Luke's International Hospital) that was seized by GHQ
during the Occupation. As the hospital was exclusively for
Occupation soldiers and their families during this period,[11]
the nurses would have been from the elite class and able

to speak English, with access to state-of-the-art US medical care. Another nurse who was falsely arrested at the same time was an English teacher at her church, and had a father who worked for the Ministry of Finance. The sixth woman was from Nagoya; she had graduated from a women's school and her father was a section manager at a major metropolitan bank. In other words, it was inconceivable that any of these women would be working as 'prostitutes'.

Here, the complaint that these women were 'mistaken for women of the dark' and were not *panpan* has a number of implications. In addition to 'discrimination against prostitutes' and the fact that they had not 'turned to the Occupation soldiers', the commentary reveals society's acceptance of evasive language such as 'discrimination against prostitutes' and 'contempt for women who have taken the side of the victors'. This is the reason that this issue was taken up by the media and put on the agenda at the National Diet. In contrast, the complaints of women who could not be considered 'model victims' were less likely to be accepted by society. As a result, the more the 'model victim' emphasized that she was not a 'woman of the dark', the more the stigma of the *panpan* was reinforced, placing such women in a situation where they found it increasingly difficult to speak out publicly.

Place descriptions: Kyoto and Kobe

In considering the sexual contact between the Occupation soldiers and the women in the occupied territories, this book focuses on Kyoto. The significance of this is twofold. Firstly, the invaluable interviews with the Japanese women who actually had sexual contact with the soldiers were conducted in Kyoto. Secondly, because the area itself was arranged according to the ranks of the soldiers (I Corps

1949), it emerged during the interview analysis that the ranks of the soldiers were linked to the social classes of the Japanese women with whom they associated. Nishikawa has highlighted the political background of the region as follows:

> Kyoto was a privileged place of comfort and rest for all of the occupying forces – not just for those stationed there, but also forces from all over the occupied territories came to Kyoto on leave. A variety of comfort facilities were built in Kyoto for the occupying forces immediately after the defeat, and there were many English-language tourist guides to Kyoto published throughout the Occupation. (Nishikawa 2017: 416)

Nishikawa also points out that Kyoto was a location that was quickly and comprehensively developed. As a result,

> Kyoto is a city with a long history of stratification of its residents. To reiterate, the military presence in the city comprised a strict class system and hierarchical divisions. The forces were a group of foreign soldiers whose language and lifestyle differed from the local residents. If we consider the Occupation space, we must, more than in other cases, look at the various human and cultural elements in combination in that space, such as gender, class, race or ethnicity, and social class, as well as the powerful influence of military actions that were at work there. (Nishikawa 2017: 238)

Thus, it is extremely important to adopt a perspective that considers the stratification of the local population in conjunction with military rank and ethnicity. The fact that the occupied city of Kyoto was 'a place of stratified comfort, rest, tourism and cultural exchange' (Nishikawa 2013: 11) also applies to the Japanese women who were the companions of Occupation soldiers. This volume brings attention to the 'voices' of these Japanese women who had sexual contact with the occupiers, which emerged in the process of focusing on Kyoto, a space where the class of occupying forces was clearly visible. It is hoped that by incorporating considerations of gender, class/hierarchy and race a more precise analysis can be achieved. While Kyoto provides the bulk of the material for analysis, in some parts of the volume, Kobe is used as a point of comparison.

The fact that occupied Kyoto was divided according to soldiers' ranks is clearly visible when compared with a map of occupied Kobe. In the case of Kobe, the facilities for commissioned officers and camps for soldiers fall within walking distance of each other (Figure 1.1), whereas in Kyoto, the officer facilities and the soldier camps are separated by Kyoto Station (Figure 1.2).

In the case of Kyoto, the distance between the segregated quarters and facilities of the soldiers and black soldiers and those for the exclusive use of officers was too great to travel on foot (Figure 1.2). There was a hotel for single officers immediately adjacent to Kyoto Station, but they traveled to the facilities in military vehicles. In Naguracho, Shimogyo ward, a little to the east of Kyoto Station, the Nihon Denchi company owned the Tsukuyomi Ryo (dormitory) which was used as a barracks for about 200 black soldiers. According to a woman who was thirty-seven at the time of the Occupation:

> Around here, it was all black soldiers. I remember their large, black faces; only their teeth were white, and their laughter. There were lots of girls – I'm not sure where they came from, but they would accompany the soldiers. Even around here, there were young women and middle-aged

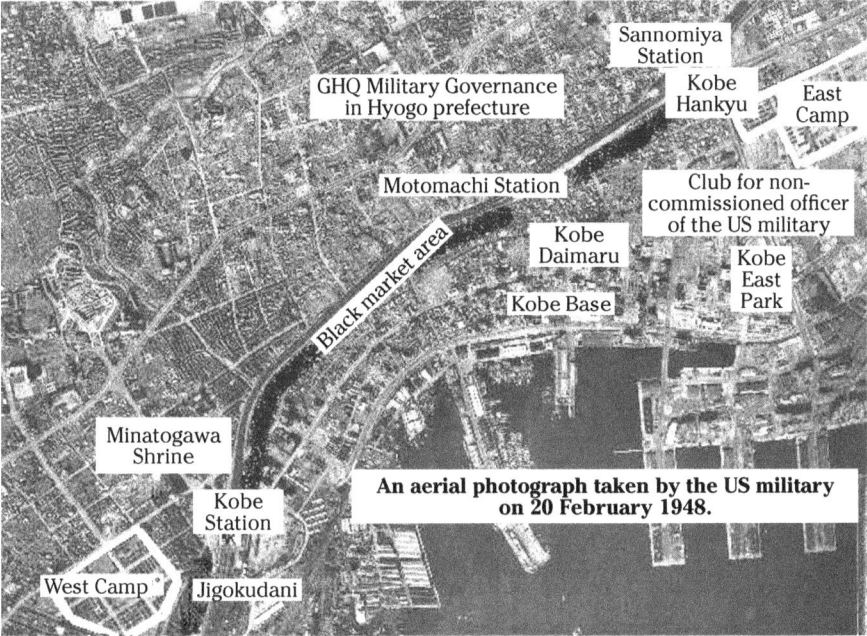

Figure 1.1 Map of occupied Kobe

> women who were having trouble making ends meet, and
> so they were behaving like *panpan*. There were mixed-race
> children with black fathers, and they would play with the
> neighborhood children. (Ryo Suzuki Seminar, College of
> Social Sciences, Ritsumeikan University, 1991; hereafter
> referred to as Ritsumeikan Suzuki Seminar)[12]

The supply corps facility where the black soldiers worked
was located right next to their barracks (I Corps 1949). The
distance from Fushimi ward, where the soldiers' camp was
located, to Kyoto Station is more than double that between
the same facilities for the Occupation forces in Kobe. The
distance from the former site of the occupying forces' West
Camp near Japan Railways (JR) Kobe Station (Figure 1.1) to
the site of the East Camp near JR Sannomiya Station (currently
in the vicinity of Loft, to the south of Kobe Hankyu) is an easy

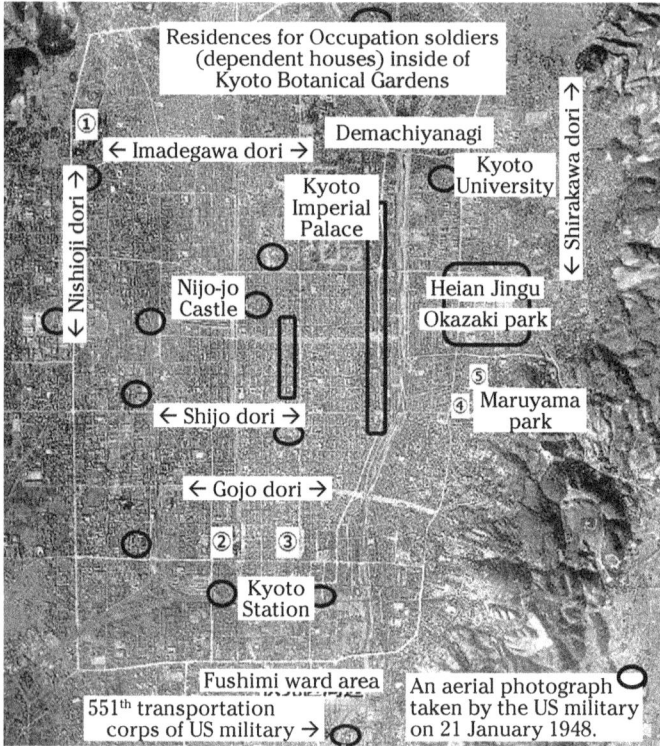

Figure 1.2
Map of occupied Kyoto

Notes: Black outlines indicate US military facilities; white outlines indicate shrines and temples, as follows: 1. Kitano Tenmangu, 2. Nishi Honganji, 3. Higashi Honganji, 4. Yasaka Jinja, 5. Chionin.

Source: The maps were prepared by the author, with reference to the CITY MAP OF KYOTO (held in the Kyoto Prefectural Archives) created by the US forces (dated 12 January 1949) and Shizue Osa's '"CITY MAP OF KYOTO" wo "Yomu": Senryoki kenkyu joron' ('Reading' the 'City Map of Kyoto': Introduction to Occupation era studies) in Chubu University's journal *Arena* (issue 15, 2013), published by Fubaisha.

*Women associating with occupying forces in and around Fushimi ward and their monthly income (blank if unknown):

Aki: 7–8,000 yen; Erika: 10,000 yen; Kasumi: 8,000 yen; Satsuki (black soldier): 10,000 yen; Haru: 5–600 yen; Lily: 400 yen per visit.

*Women associating with occupying forces outside Fushimi ward and their monthly income (blank if unknown):

Ai: 12,000 yen; Aoi: 15–20,000 yen; Asa: 30–40,000 yen; Azami: 30,000 yen; Anzu: 15,000 yen; Umeko: 20,000 yen; Kaede: 15,000 yen; Sakura: 400 yen per visit; Satsuki: 10,000 yen; Shion: 10,000 yen; Shunka: 20–30,000 yen; Tamako: 6,000 yen;

Tsukushi: 30–50,000 yen; Tsubaki: 30,000 yen; Hamana: 40,000 yen; Matsuko: 25,000 yen; Mayu: 10,000 yen; Mari: 7,000 yen per week; Mina: 10,000 yen; Mokuren: 45,000 yen; Yukiko: 10–30,000 yen; Yuzu: 25,000 yen; Yotsuba: 6,000 yen; Ran: 20,000 yen; Rira: 5–8,000 yen; Rin: 10,000 yen; Ruri: 10,000 yen; Waka: 9,000 yen; Sara: 12,000 yen; Nanoka: 5 yen once every two months.

*In order to examine the relationship between the ranks of the occupying forces and their deployment in Kyoto, only those women who stated the amount of money they received per month from the occupying forces are listed.

walk even for female junior and senior high school students. In Kobe, although the camps were differentiated by race, with the West and East housing black and white soldiers respectively, once they stepped out of the camps, the groups were within walking distance of each other. However, in Kyoto, the facilities for the officers were clustered around the vicinity of Heian Jingu, which is a considerable walk from Kyoto Station. To reiterate, the occupying forces' facilities in Kyoto were delineated according to rank, a situation that was totally different to that in Kobe, where regardless of rank or race, the forces were able to walk around easily. If we look at the residences of the women discussed in this volume by placing them on a map of Kyoto (Figure 1.2), it becomes clear that in Fushimi ward, the so-called 'exclusive' women who associated with one specific man generally received less than 10,000 yen per month (and none received more than 20,000 per month), indicating that the sexual partners of the women in this ward were mainly soldiers. The cases of Hana, Nobara, Yuri and Natsuko, whose names are not listed under the map, are exceptional ones. Although Hana and Nobara earned more than 10,000 yen per month, they were both 'butterflies' (women who interacted with an unspecified number of Occupation soldiers), and it is not clear how many sexual partners they had per month. In Yuri's case, she did not specify whether she had her own dressmaking shop in Fushimi ward separate to her house, or how much she received per month from the Occupation soldier to whom she was engaged. In spite of occasional exceptions, where soldiers could afford to give more than 30,000 yen per month for sexual companionship, monthly earnings only exceeded this level in the case of 'prostitution' and never amongst women living in Fushimi ward. One exceptional case outside Fushimi ward was that of Natsuko, who lived in Shijo

Matsubara and was dating a soldier (twenty-two years old). The soldier visited Natsuko's lodgings only on the weekends, and returned to base around 9pm, so Natsuko was able to continue dating him without having to live in Fushimi.

In terms of the rank and pay of the occupying forces, there was a large disparity between the officers and the soldiers. Therefore, the amount of pay received by the women associating with the forces varied according to their rank and their own needs for supplies and cash. In September 1947, a twenty-five-year-old military physician (officer) by the name of John D. Grisman was posted to Kyoto as the head of the Public Health Section in the Kyoto Military Government. His superior was Colonel Crawford F. Sams, the director of Public Health and Welfare mentioned above. Sams was also superior to the head of the Welfare Section, Emily Putnam, a social worker who advised on the investigation into 'street prostitutes' discussion in this volume. Grisman and Putnam were colleagues in different sections. The historian Sei Nishimura has painted a picture of occupied Kyoto from Grisman's perspective using letters and color photographs sent by Grisman to his parents at home (Nishimura 2015).

According to Grisman's letters, a soldier's monthly salary was US$20, but his own salary as a newly appointed military physician was US$160 (Nishimura 2015: 42). The women's narratives recorded in *Streetwalkers* are from around 1948; calculating 270 yen to the dollar that year, as an officer, Grisman's monthly salary, even if he was paid the minimum wage, would have been around 43,200 yen. Assuming Grisman's 'twenty dollars per month for soldiers' description is correct, then their corresponding monthly salary would have been 5,400 yen.

In 1948, the starting monthly salary for a primary school teacher was 2,000 yen (*Shukan Asahi*, ed., 1995: 102), while in

2015, a university graduate primary school teacher's starting monthly salary was 201,900 yen,[13] a difference of about 100 times. Applying this multiplier to Grisman's 1948 monthly salary to convert it to today's currency value amounts to 4,320,000 yen. Even as a soldier, his monthly salary would have been 540,000 yen. Even though a soldier's monthly salary was an eighth of an officer's, soldiers stationed in occupied territories were paid more than double the starting salary of a primary school teacher.

Considering that Grisman's monthly salary of US$160 was a starting salary for a newly appointed military physician, his pay would have increased commensurate with his experience. In March 1949, Grisman was told that 'if he became a subordinate of Director Sams at GHQ, his monthly salary would increase three-fold to US$775' (Nishimura 2015: 300), meaning that at that point, his salary was approximately US$259 (or 69,750 yen).

Furthermore, Grisman's father had been a doctor in the US Navy during World War I (Nishimura 2015: 63), and his mother was a social worker (Nishimura 2015: 187). Grisman frequently requested that his mother send Christmas presents to his Japanese colleagues (Nishimura 2015: 51–52). In other words, because Grisman was single and was brought up in an elite social class, he was free to spend all of his salary in Japan on himself. Grisman's case demonstrates that the more important one's position in the Occupation forces was, the easier it was to pay sexual partners around 20–30,000 yen per month and even cohabit with them, meaning that they had a degree of freedom in terms of finances and leisure not afforded to regular soldiers.

However, as Grisman wrote in a letter to his parents, 'A dollar is worth between 400 and 800 yen, and even the US soldiers' underwear was worth around 500 yen' (Nishimura

2015: 25). Because a dollar was worth more than the fixed exchange rate of 270 yen, even a soldier's monthly salary of US$20 was, in reality, worth between 8,000 and 16,000 yen. Nevertheless, even taking this into account, if a member of the occupying forces was able to hand over more than 30,000 yen per month to a sexual partner, he must have been part of the officer class.

Highlighting the wage discrepancy, Virginia Ohlson, who arrived from the US in May 1947 to work as a nurse, was paid twice the annual salary she earned at home, and 'was able to afford a Japanese maid to clean her hotel room. She had no objections to her pay, her lifestyle, or her position' (Ohishi 2004: 101). As part of the military, life in occupied Japan was also good for Ohlson.

As we will see in the ensuing chapters, this wage gap was reflected in the social class of the Japanese women who worked as sexual partners for the occupying forces. There was a tendency for the Japanese women from higher social classes to have close relationships with the military's officer class. Furthermore, the analysis reveals that the social class of the Japanese women working as sexual partners can be inferred from whether the monthly payment was above or below 10,000 yen. The places of residence for women accompanying occupying forces were also not unrelated to the amount of money they received, as demonstrated by Figure 1.2. Furthermore, there were cases of women from higher social class backgrounds dating soldiers on the premise that it would lead to marriage. These were not exceptional cases, but they were one result of the overwhelming power asymmetry of the Occupation, as will be discussed in the chapters that follow.

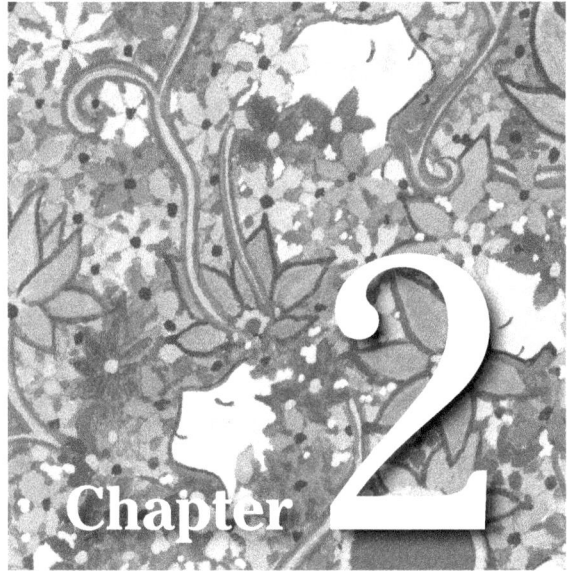

Chapter 2

Strategies for
Surviving Rape

This chapter examines indisputably sexually violent encounters between Occupation soldiers and women in occupied territories and uses the concept of the contact zone to highlight three examples of how women in occupied territories showed resilience in the face of rape. The behavior of each of these women after being raped was a survival strategy.

There were no limits to how Occupation soldiers could treat the defeated population and they experienced few repercussions for their behavior. In Kyoto, for example, a soldier who ran over a Japanese citizen in a traffic accident would barely be punished, while the victim

> was personally responsible for preparing documents, such as proof of the accident issued by the local police chief; doctor's certificates and invoices for home repair work; applying for compensation for the financial difficulties caused by the accident by submitting a form to the Kyoto Prefectural Office's liaison division; and waiting for the money to be paid from Japanese treasury funds that were earmarked for expenses relating to the war defeat. (Nishikawa 2013: 6)

In other words, damage claims for traffic accidents were made in an environment characterized by the overwhelmingly asymmetric power relationship that was the Occupation. Anyone wishing to file a claim had to go to great lengths to get past the 'many barriers that stood between them and lodging an application' (Nishikawa 2017: 91). Moreover, 'Accident-related damage claims did not include sexual crimes' (Nishikawa 2017: 242).

As mentioned earlier, GHQ's Criminal Investigation Division (CID) reported sexual crimes perpetrated by Occupation soldiers, together with other crimes such as robbery and brawling, in their Weekly Summary of Events. Sexual crimes were reported with increasing frequency immediately after the outbreak of the Korean War. Rapes that were committed by soldiers in occupied territories and then reported in the CID's weekly summary broadly followed one of three patterns.

In the first pattern, the rape was discovered and an investigation opened after the perpetrator returned to his military base covered in blood. For example, when a severely intoxicated private first class (PFC) returned to his base wearing a bloodied t-shirt at around 8pm on 1 August 1950, the subsequent investigation found that he had raped a sixteen-year-old girl at a temple near her home.

The second pattern involved persons other than the victim reporting a rape at a *koban* (neighborhood police station) or other Japanese police authority. One such incident occurred on the evening of 13 May 1950, when an unknown airman abducted two fifteen-year-old girls. One girl managed to escape, but while she was reporting the incident at a *koban*, the other girl had been raped. In a similar case in Kumamoto at 11:50pm on 13 June 1950, the perpetrator was a soldier who was known to the victim's older sister. He had visited their home and, finding the younger sister alone, raped her. When the victim's sister returned, she found blood under her sister's clothes. She questioned her sister, who told her that she had been raped. A third example of this pattern of rape happened on 3 August 1950. A married couple was walking along a street near Shinagawa when a black soldier dragged the wife away and raped her. The victim's husband ran to the Japanese police for help, and the military police (MP) caught the perpetrator fleeing into a private house.

The third pattern involved the victim self-reporting their rape to authorities such as the police. Rapes that followed this pattern were also reported in the CID's Weekly Summary of Events via reports from the Japanese police that passed through the MP. Cases that fit this pattern are discussed later in this chapter.

We must not forget that Occupation soldiers were armed. In a rape that occurred in Tokyo on 2 July 1950, a girl (aged ten) was playing with her younger brother when she was abducted and raped in a car. The pair of soldiers who attacked her each carried a .45 caliber handgun.[1] The girl was thrown out of the car after being raped, and witnesses who saw her sobbing and crying reported the incident to the police.

It is also important to note that several records in the CID's weekly publication blatantly discriminated against prostitutes. One example of this was a sexual assault that took place in a building in suburban Kyoto at approximately 4:30pm on 28 April 1950. Two unknown airmen forced their way into the twenty-two-year-old victim's room, beat her, and raped her. Two women (both aged nineteen) in the same building heard her cries and came running but were kept out of her room by three other unknown airmen, who beat and raped them. The report noted that the five suspects could not be identified, and that the investigation was therefore continuing using lineups of airmen in the area. The report also noted that the building where the victims lived was a 'house of ill repute', and that the assaulted women were also 'notorious prostitutes'. GHQ worked actively to eliminate VDs and assumed that 'houses of ill repute' were detestable *panpan* houses, or brothels, that targeted Occupation soldiers. To GHQ, such houses ought not to have existed. This report differed from others in that it identified the victims as prostitutes. Other women were only identified by their full name and age. Regardless of whether the victims were prostitutes or not, the forced entry of five unknown airmen into the building and their battery and rape of three women was undeniably a sex crime. The case also illustrates the position in which Japanese women found themselves in the overwhelmingly asymmetric violence that was perpetrated in occupied territories.

If a resident of a defeated country struggled to file charges for so much as a traffic accident, how much more effort would a victim of rape have needed to expend to self-report her experience to the police and other authorities? The real cases examined in the first two parts of this chapter involve reports made to GHQ from the victim's side, the outcomes of which frustrated rapists' plans. In the third part of this chapter, I discuss women who were not 'model victims' of sexual assault. Each of these cases illustrate survival strategies used by women in occupied territories who were raped by Occupation soldiers.

With that in mind, what were these survival strategies?

Self-reported rape: Kogiku, Seri and Suzuna's survival strategy

In each of these three cases, the victim self-reported being raped. If we use the concept of the contact zone to examine the overwhelmingly asymmetric power relationship that existed between the soldiers as perpetrators of sexual violence and the Japanese women who were their victims, we can see that self-reported rape was significant in that the accusation came from the side of the less-powerful. These women were, however, identified only by their age and where they were from, and not by the additional label of 'prostitute'.

The first case[2] involves Kogiku (aged twenty-two), who was traveling from Numazu to Osaka on a Japanese-only train on 8 June 1950, when an unknown Occupation soldier

53

approached her and forced her into the train's toilet. The soldier propositioned her, and when Kogiku refused, he grabbed her face and slapped her until she yielded, before raping her. After Kogiku reported the incident to a railway worker, CID authorities boarded the train at Osaka at 6:15am the following morning and apprehended the suspect. Kogiku had multiple scratches and bruises to her face and head and was taken to a US military hospital in Osaka. By reporting her assault to the railway worker, and through her involvement in the arrest of the soldier who assaulted her, Kogiku was able to be examined at a well-equipped hospital that catered exclusively to the occupying army.

The second case[3] concerns a seventeen-year-old named Seri. She was walking along a street in Osaka at about 8:30pm on 11 June 1950, when two soldiers (both nineteen-year-old PFCs) raped her on the lawn by the nearby warehouse they were guarding. Seri reported her rape to the Japanese police, who then reported it to the MP. This experience – self-reporting her assault, knowing that the MP arrested the two soldiers under suspicion of rape, and having the incident reported in the Weekly Summary of Events – would doubtless have proved to Seri that victims of rape did not have to remain silent.

The final case[4] occurred in Tokyo, one week after the outbreak of the Korean War. Suzuna (age unknown) was raped on 5 July 1950, 100 yards (approximately ninety-one meters) from the main entrance to the US military base in Tokyo. She was walking along a side road near the base, when two soldiers from the 71st Signal Service Battalion grabbed her, dragged her between two barracks, and raped her. One of the rapists had climbed a utility pole to remove its light before the assault. After being raped, Suzuna was taken to the main entrance of the base. She reported her rape at the Azabu Police Station and was treated at a hospital. Authorities found the soldier's fingerprints on the removed streetlight and interviewed around fifty-one members of the 71st Signal Service Battalion who were in the area at the time of the assault. According to Shin Aoki, who researched jazz musicians who came to Japan with the Occupation forces, the living quarters of the battalion in question were near Hibiya Park (Aoki 2013: 26–27). This suggests that Suzuna was probably assaulted near that park. Identifying features of the soldiers who raped Suzuna were absent from the CID's Weekly Summary of Events. The record noted that investigations were ongoing as of 5 July, when Suzuna was assaulted, but what happened subsequently is unclear.

The climbing of the utility pole and the removal of the streetlight are evidence of pre-meditation, and clearly show that this pair of soldiers planned their crime more carefully than the warehouse guards who assaulted Seri. Yet their attempt to conceal their crime was undermined when Suzuna reported her rape to the police. While we do not know how Suzuna's report was ultimately resolved, the perpetrators were obviously expecting her to remain silent. They were soldiers from a victorious country; Suzuna was a woman from a defeated one. Moreover, given the stigma of being a rape victim, it would have been no surprise if Suzuna had suffered in silence. Suzuna's refusal to do so, and her decision to report her rape, are demonstrably a survival strategy.

Reported by her older brother: Mokuren's survival strategy

When rape victims revealed that Occupation soldiers had assaulted them, they were not always supported by their families. This was the case for Aoi (aged seventeen) and

Sakurako (aged twenty-one). Aoi, who was completing a traineeship at a hospital in Okayama, was returning home late one evening when a pair of soldiers assaulted her. 'They stole my virginity. I was shocked, heartbroken, and I just sat there in the darkness, crying for two hours', said Aoi. Later, 'I told my aunt everything, but she got angry. She told me I needed to support myself, so I moved out'.

Like Aoi, Sakurako was also assaulted on her way home. Sakurako worked as a nurse, and despite being 'dressed modestly, in my plain, navy-blue work uniform, my hair plainly styled [i.e., without a fashionable perm]', she was dragged into a *machiai* (the old equivalent of a 'love hotel') at around 9pm and raped by a pair of soldiers. When the soldiers had grabbed her, Sakurako says that she had resisted with all her might: 'I shouted and struggled, but nobody noticed'. After she told her 'moralistic' father what had happened, their relationship soured and Sakurako, like Aoi, left home.

Sakurako and Aoi's accounts were similar in that they were both 'model victims' of rape (Ueno [1998] 2012). A 'model victim' of rape is a sexual innocent who can claim to have vehemently resisted being assaulted. When Aoi spoke of how 'they shoved a handkerchief into my mouth when I screamed', how she resisted fiercely, and when she used expressions such as 'They stole my virginity. I was shocked, heartbroken', she stressed her sexual purity. Sakurako was likewise adamant that there was nothing provocative about her physical appearance, and that she did all she could to resist. The responses of both Aoi and Sakurako show that even if women were raped by Occupation soldiers, the patriarchal system in which they lived meant that they were blamed for being assaulted, and that not only did this shame their families, but it also turned these women into 'damaged goods' whom nobody would accept as brides.[5] 'Model victim' or not, both Aoi and Sakurako were rejected by their families.

Unlike victims who experienced such rejection, when Mokuren (aged twenty) told her family that an Occupation soldier had raped her, her older brother furiously reported the assault to the US military. On an October evening immediately following the war, soldiers abducted Mokuren (then aged sixteen) in a truck as she was returning home. According to Mokuren:

> [NAME REDACTED] came in a medium-sized truck and forced me inside. I'd long heard rumors that the soldiers would kill you if you shouted or struggled, so I was shaking, terrified. A woman was in the truck, and we were both taken to a hotel. There were three [REDACTED] and three women there. I was so naïve that I thought you could get pregnant from kissing, so of course I didn't know what it meant to be with a man. The next day, they bundled me back into the truck, took me away, and raped me.

After being abducted in a truck on her way home and raped, Mokuren was made to cook and do other chores at the soldiers' camp, before being taken back to the hotel. Mokuren's older brother and mother, anxious that she had not come home the night before, started searching for her at various *ryokan* (Japanese inns), before finally finding the hotel where she was being held. When Mokuren told her older brother what had happened, he furiously filed a complaint with the US military. As a result, the soldiers who raped Mokuren were punished and sent home two months later, near the beginning of 1946. That Mokuren's mother and older brother had immediately started searching *ryokan* after she had failed to return home indicates that soldiers forcibly abducting Japanese women, taking them to *ryokan* or hotels, and assaulting them there was a common occurence in occupied territories.

In Mokuren's case, far from being rejected by her mother and older brother, her older brother filed a complaint with the US military that led to the punishment of Mokuren's rapists. Unlike Seri and Suzuna, the day after she was raped, Mokuren was forced to 'help prepare food at the camp', before being taken back to the hotel. Mokuren was not able to escape the soldiers, but if she had directly reported her rape to GHQ, they would likely have asked her why she had not simply run away from the perpetrators. In other words, Mokuren must have sensed that they would not have taken her self-reported claims seriously. Instead, she succeeded in having her older brother report the rape.

Survival strategies for women who were not 'model victims'

Of the sixty-three women focused on in this study who participated in the *Streetwalkers* survey, only seven – including Aoi and Sakurako, discussed earlier – told investigators that they were raped by Occupation soldiers. These seven women were 'model victims', and this was what allowed them to report the assaults. Unlike other forms of violence, victims of sexual assault do not always, or cannot always, speak of their experience. This is because, if they are not a 'model victim', they are less likely to be taken at their word. Women who associated with multiple soldiers were particularly likely to be held responsible for being raped. Even if the victim was a 'model victim', she could still be rejected by her family (as Aoi and Sakurako were). Others, such as Mina (aged nineteen), 'became a *panpan* girl out of desperation, after I was raped'. There were also women, including Sakurako, who 'made a living by scrounging up [REDACTED], here and there', prostituting themselves to Occupation soldiers because they were raped. Mühlhäuser notes that, in Russia and other countries during World War II, 'a woman who was raped lost the cultural ascription of innocence and was considered to be spiritually and morally compromised' (2020: 43). In Japan, too, a woman who was raped was immediately stigmatized as a 'tainted woman', regardless of whether she was a 'model victim'. Mina and Sakurako's arguably 'desperate' behavior after being raped reflect this stigmatization. In a world that was unwilling to accept them, when women who were not 'model victims' exerted their agency after being raped, how did they behave?

Women who were not 'model victims' sometimes solicited money from the soldiers who assaulted them. This featured in the reports that Anne (aged nineteen), Fuyuko (aged nineteen) and Nana (aged twenty) gave to investigators.

Anne met an Occupation soldier while working as a 'dancer' in a cabaret in Osaka.[6] The soldier tricked her and took her to a *ryokan*, where her 'virginity was stolen'. According to Anne, 'I didn't know you could be paid for that, so of course I wasn't'.

In Fuyuko's case, she was walking with a friend near Umeda Station when Occupation soldiers grabbed them, drove them to a hotel, and raped Fuyuko. The two were then driven back to Umeda Station, and a crying Fuyuko went to her friend's house. Her friend said nothing at the time, but Fuyuko later learned that she had also been raped. 'I knew nothing', said Fuyuko. 'I didn't ask [NAME REDACTED] for money, I didn't even know that I could'.

Both Anne and Fuyuko's accounts show that women who were assaulted by soldiers would often solicit money from their rapists. However, as they had never been raped before, both women stated that they did not know that they were able to ask for money after being raped – the implication being that women who did solicit money had been raped by Occupation soldiers on multiple occasions.

The next account, by Nana, suggests that soldiers implicitly acknowledged the need to pay the women that they raped in occupied territories. This understanding was perhaps driven by the desire to prevent victims from reporting their assault to the police or to other authorities. After all, as examples like Suzuna's assault show, even though the pair of soldiers raped her only after executing a careful plan that involved removing the light from a utility pole, Suzuna still went to the police.

Nana was on her way to visit a friend at around 7pm when an Occupation soldier grabbed her, and 'popped her cherry' in the classroom of a nearby school. He then tried asking her for her name and address, before giving her his name. Some days later, as Nana got off a train, she saw the soldier who had assaulted her making his way towards her, and she ran. Nana later learned that the man had been trying to give her money.

Anne, Fuyuko and Nana's accounts thus demonstrate not only how women in occupied territories solicited money from the soldiers who raped them, but also how some of these soldiers agreed to pay their victims. In other words, there was a tacit understanding between the soldier who committed the rape and the victimized woman that money would be exchanged after the assault. It is nevertheless important to stress that these rapes occurred within the confines of an overwhelmingly asymmetric relationship of power. This is highlighted by accounts such as that of Nana: 'I cried for help, but even though people passed, even though they saw me, nobody came'. Occupation soldiers who perpetrated the rapes undoubtedly gave their victims money in an attempt to transform the rape into sex work, but for their victims, the monetization of their experience did not erase the reality that they had been raped. Even once victims 'learned' how to respond and began soliciting money before being assaulted instead of after, there was no changing the reality that the assault itself was still 'paid rape'. This solicitation of money was therefore arguably a way for rape victims to object to both the unassailable violence perpetrated by soldiers and a society in which only the word of a 'model victim' was taken seriously. In other words, this monetization was itself a survival strategy that women who were not 'model victims' employed in the contact zone where Occupation soldiers encountered women in occupied territories.

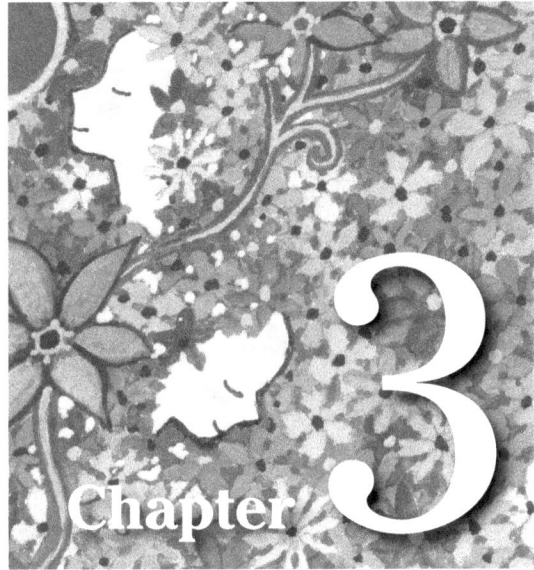

Chapter 3

Sex Work
Survival Strategies:
Sponsored by
Occupation
Soldiers

Prostitution, besides being found in the usual 'whorehouses', was supported by the Occupation forces in bases with special military lodgings for women, hotels where single senior officers stayed and where, according to eighteen-year-old Sara, evening parties were held. The below case of one night of sex work with a high-ranking officer demonstrates the substantial asymmetry between women who sold their services to Occupation soldiers and the soldiers who bought them.

Twenty-three-year-old Botan, who had a three-year-old daughter, helped out with chores at home for a while after graduating from S girls' high school in Osaka, but her family was poor. Her older sister introduced her to geisha life, and she acquired a patron who supported her during the war. She gave birth to her daughter in 1945. By this time her father had died, as had her only older brother and the sister who had recommended that she become a geisha. After the war ended, Botan went with her mother and daughter to Kyoto and lived on a lane adjacent to the eastern side of the Kyoto Hotel. In Botan's words:

> I had liaisons with [NAME REDACTED] at the hotel near our tenement but only ever received sweets or chocolates. I'd display a kimono collar, kimono or obi sash. Hotel guests would throw chocolates down from the windows and, if they liked an obi they were shown, they'd come down for it, so trade flourished around the lane.

At that time all the senior officers, whether single or family men, were housed in the best hotels in Japan. According to the City Map of Kyoto (CMK) held in the Kyoto Prefectural Library and Archives, which was produced by GHQ to show various US military facilities, Kyoto Hotel, marked as 'Civilian Officers' Billets', was for the use of civilian attachés as well as military officers. The CMK map, dated 12 January 1949, accords with the memoirs of women of the period reported in *Streetwalkers*, and Kyoto Hotel was to the southeast of the old imperial palace and within walking distance of the offices of high-class members of the Occupation forces. An understanding of the scarcity of goods at the time and of the fact that 'interactions between Occupation forces and civilians were stratified' (Nishikawa 2013: 33) indicates the status of the people with whom the officers bartered through the hotel windows. They were of a class that had access to kimonos and *obis* despite straitened circumstances.

As Botan explains,

> High-ranking officers came to the neighborhood for entertainment. One of them, Officer W, invited me to a hotel, which was unusual, so I agreed to go. I spent the night in his top-notch room and slept with him. The next morning, before I left, he gave me chocolates and some other gifts for my child. I didn't see him again after that.

This elite officer who so lightly dispensed with Botan after having sex with her in free accommodation also bestowed 'gifts' upon her the next morning, items that were virtually free to such officers. Botan made no mention of receiving any money from him, so not only did the officer apparently have the benefit of sharing his free room with her for the night, he also gave her gifts that he did not need to pay for. Besides showing how an officer could enjoy a free one-night stand, the case demonstrates some of the blatant power imbalances of occupied Japan that were based on background and class.

Japan was not the only country where food supplies and other necessities were exchanged for sex during a military occupation. The same held true in the occupied territories of World War II for German soldiers stationed in the German-occupied Soviet Union who used local women in similar ways: 'In view of the catastrophic food situation during the war, it was often possible for members of the Wehrmachat and SS to offer food or other vital goods in exchange for sexual satisfaction' (Mühlhäuser 2020: 305). In liberated France, too, 'Many female civilians who were not prostitutes also engaged in sex for certain products' (Roberts 2013: 127).

Women in occupied territories managed to survive the vast imbalances by exchanging sex for items that were trivial to occupation soldiers. If we interpret this from the perspective of the contact zone of sex work however, the women were not being unilaterally exploited by the occupation soldiers. Below, I demonstrate how they were making full use of their agency within the means available to them.

Shion: sponsoring debts to a first lover (occupying solider)

Eighteen-year-old Shion had relationships with three Occupation soldiers, of which the first and third are taken up in this discussion. The second can be omitted as Shion 'dropped him because of his drinking'. Of course, Shion's decision to discontinue her relationship with a 'drinker' could also be considered as part of her survival strategy.

Shion's educational background is unclear, but she was living by herself at the time in a boarding house in Kawabata, Sakyo ward, in Kyoto. Her two older brothers, who were office workers, and her older sister and two younger brothers all lived together; however, as Shion did not get on well with her older brothers, she had lived until recently with her younger sister who worked in the textile industry. Her father, who had died from a cerebral hemorrhage when she was fourteen, had worked in the timber industry, so while he was alive they had probably been well off. Her mother died from a gastrointestinal illness two years after her father's demise. Although Shion calls the twenty-five-year-old Occupation soldier she was first intimate with her 'first lover', he took advantage of her.

> I lost my virginity to [NAME REDACTED] in July last year (1948). […] I loved him but dropped him after discovering he was two-timing me with another woman.

The only reason Shion became involved with a third soldier was 'to pay back the money I owed to my first lover'. Once the debt was paid, she hoped 'to marry a good twenty-four-or-five-year-old Japanese man'. She clearly only thought of the third soldier as a sponsor to pay off her debts.

Shion reported that she 'only received 5,000 yen a month' from this third man, but because he also supplied her with food and clothes, this extra was worth about 10,000 yen 'cash' to her. This soldier came to Shion every day so he must have been a relatively high-ranking officer who had free time and could easily get away from work. Since he only gave Shion 5,000 yen per month, he may have sent the rest of his pay to his family back home.

Shion was shrewd in her reliance on this soldier for financial reasons. Furthermore, even though they only had sex three times a week, he visited Shion every day, indicating that he still came to see her regardless of the sex. The contact zone between Shion and this third man was thus a space in which she engaged in order to repay her debt to the first soldier.

Sakura: not a *'panpan* girl' but using a pimp

Unlike Shion, nineteen-year-old Sakura had countless Occupation soldier customers at the hotel. After she graduated from a girls' high school in Hiroshima, she worked in a spinning company in Kobe city as part of the service volunteer corps. After losing both parents to the A-bomb, she was evacuated to her mother's home town of Matsue in Shimane prefecture where her two younger brothers had already been sent. Her uncle was too strict for Sakura though, so in 1947 she left for the 'unburnt city', Kyoto, to work in a café. Later, she wanted to return to her uncle's house and stayed there for a year but it 'wasn't any fun', so she came back to Kyoto where she bumped into a co-worker from the café and, through her, took up with the Occupation soldiers.

> I took a live-in job at K Café opposite a shoe shop on Shijo-Yamatooji, earning 1,500 yen a month working there during the day, but it wasn't enough, so I began taking on customers at a hotel in Kawabata through a pimp. It was 1,500 yen for the night and 600 yen a time. I made 400 out of the 600 as 200 yen went on the room. For overnight stays, out of the 1,500 yen, I only pocketed 1,100 as I had to pay 400 for the room.

At that time, 400 yen was the going rate for sex with an Occupation soldier. Twenty-three-year-old Lily, who worked with Occupation soldiers at a brothel in Fushimi ward, also mentioned that she 'only made about 400 yen a time because the madame took 200 yen out of the 600'. Fushimi had a base camp for enlisted soldiers, and although Lily's evidence demonstrates that there was a difference between enlisted soldiers and officers, the girls working in brothels all earned the same fee.

Moreover, Sakura's narrative shows that at this time, women from the regions who left their parents' homes had to take on more than one job in order to be able to survive. In those days, if you were not 'registered' you could not receive rations,[1] so you would have to buy goods on the overpriced black market. Sakura's day job at the café where she lived was not enough for instance, so she cleverly made use of a pimp to access Occupation soldiers to supplement the shortfall in her living expenses. Through this, the investigator recorded Sakura as appearing to be 'an upright character'.

Out of the sixty-three women's stories in this analysis, Sakura and twenty-five-year-old Matsuko were the only women who mentioned pimps. In contrast with Sakura, Matsuko was recorded as: (1) having no concept of chastity; (2) being a fully-fledged *panpan*; and (3) having no overt sense of shame. She had a child to the Occupation soldier with whom she lived and received 25,000 yen a month from him but, even though this was quite a substantial amount, she said she could not live on it and therefore took on customers at a *panpan* house through pimps. She said she had been hospitalized several times with a VD and that it was so expensive that she had to continue to earn even after she was released from hospital. She added that in order to work as a prostitute she had to pay someone '3,000 yen a month for childcare for her three-year-old' and 'often had to buy treats and other goods'. Moreover, she felt exploited by the *panpan* house, which extracted money from her in other ways such as for cleaning and laundry. Matsuko complained that her life was 'hard – not as easy as other people imagine it to be'.

While the investigator judged Matsuko to be 'a fully-fledged *panpan*' due to her lack of shame at her involvement in the sex industry, Sakura was considered 'upright' because her financial difficulties had forced her into sex work, even though she used hotels and pimps just as Matsuko did. This judgement appears to be more about their different 'characters' than about their work as '*panpan*' per se.

In spite of both Sakura and Matsuko telling the investigator that they needed to use brothels and pimps to earn enough money to live, the investigator formed completely different views of them based on the fact that Sakura did not disclose her monthly income, while Matsuko told them that she prostituted herself while receiving a large sum of money from the Occupation soldier with whom she lived. By saying, 'I'd like a proper job and, if I find a good partner, I want to get married', Sakura ensured the investigator knew that she wanted to be 'rehabilitated'. That is, her narrative takes a completely different stance from that of Matsuko who only talks about how she gets through everyday life. Whereas Matsuko's story conveys a sense of urgency about not having enough money, Sakura's narrative does not, suggesting that her survival strategy of making a living through sex work was successful. After this interview, even if Sakura returned to café work by day and sex work with Occupation soldiers by night, she would still have been recorded as a woman with the potential to start a new life. Matsuko, on the other hand, used her parenting as a survival strategy, which will be discussed in Chapter 8.

Suzu: from prostitute in the red-light district to exclusive prostitute to an Occupation soldier

In contrast with Shion and Sakura, twenty-three-year-old Suzu was a woman who worked in the red-light district from before the war. After her carpenter-father took ill and could no longer work, finances and relations with her step-mother deteriorated, so she was sold off to a brothel soon after she finished elementary school. Suzu's evidence makes it clear that some women were not only sent off to red-light districts due to poverty, but also because of strained relationships with family members. Although Suzu was from Kobe, due to age restrictions there, she was sent to work in Kagoshima. The Kagoshima brothel did not attract many customers however, so after two years she, along with her debt, moved to the Shinmachi red-light area in Osaka. When the brothel at Shinmachi became war damaged, Suzu moved to another brothel in the red-light area in Tobita, Osaka, and remained there until the war ended. In the autumn of 1945, the Occupation soldiers visited this brothel, and Suzu ended up resigning from her job to take up residence with one of these men until he returned home two years later.

The important point here is that the reason Suzu was able to leave the brothel was that she persuaded an Occupation soldier to cover her bond payment, releasing her from her obligation to work at the establishment. She had already initiated a similar release from the Kagoshima brothel by orchestrating the move to Shinmachi in Osaka after realizing the lack of income potential in Kagoshima and making a 'request for a referral'. Even though Suzu was subject to a system of increasing debts in the red-light scene, the main reason she could move to more reasonable working conditions or take up with an Occupation soldier was her

71

self-motivation and ability to take the initiative within the limits available to her.

Besides being able to take such action, Suzu targeted an Occupation soldier who looked as though he could afford to secure her release. There must have been a plethora of such soldiers who visited the brothel, but Suzu was able to leave because she found a candidate who had the potential and will to extricate her, even if he was not her favorite. Suzu's survival strategy not only enabled her to ignite the romantic emotions of an Occupation soldier who had the economic means to extricate her, but it also helped her acquire an extraordinary sponsor, a soldier from the victor's side.

Nobara: children as part of her survival strategy

Thirty-six-year-old Nobara entertained Occupation clients at her home in Fushimi where she lived with the four children she had with her husband, then interned in Siberia. According to Nobara, all the children – one boy and three girls – were formally registered and 'weren't overly concerned about the way I was living'. Their ages are unknown, but judging by Nobara's age and the fact that the Occupation soldiers bought them toys, they must have been quite young.

Because of her husband's internment, initially Nobara was eligible for the military pension under the Military Aid Law. According to Megumi Kanagawa (2012: 5), this pension was quite generous: 'For bereaved military families, there were special protections and benefits such as tax exemptions; special dormitories for mothers and children; reductions or exemptions for school admission and tuition fees; provision of education supplies and school lunches; and preferential employment privileges'. Aside from this pension, Nobara took a job in a travel agency for which she received 3,500 yen per month. Considering that the starting salary for an elementary school teacher at the time was 2,000 yen per month, 3,500 yen would amount to about 350,000 yen in today's currency. The level of her salary implies that the job required English competency. From September 1946, however, when the Military Aid Law was abolished and replaced by the former Public Assistance Law, which stated that 'those with an income of 3,000 yen or more are not entitled to receive the pension', Nobara was no longer eligible for the military pension. This legislative change meant that she now had to pay for all items that had previously been exempted from payment. Because 3,500 yen a month was not enough to support her family of five, Nobara took on Occupation soldier customers at home.

Nobara was also well acquainted with the welfare system through the district officers she knew. She complained that 'they didn't look after us properly and only judged us by public rumours, so were negative towards us'. At that time, the welfare officers were appointed by GHQ,[2] which disapproved of sex work, so it was the norm for women like Nobara to be neglected.

Nobara reported, 'I chose a path that could support me and my children and allow them to go to school'. She had no idea when her husband would return home from the war; for Nobara and her four children to be able to survive and stay together, sex work with Occupation soldiers became the main source of revenue for the family. Her parents had passed away, and she gave no indication as to other relatives, including on her husband's side. According to her, she had no-one else to rely on financially while her husband was away. She was a single mother whose government aid had been cut, so it seems unreasonable for anyone to judge her for resorting to sex work with Occupation soldiers to enable her family to survive during the Occupation.

Also of note here are Nobara's appeals to her Occupation soldier customers regarding her four children. Among the sixty-three women analyzed in this study, Nobara is the only one who mentioned liaising with Occupation soldiers in a house with children present. Her report that these customers 'bought toys etc. for the children' suggests that they were not too concerned about the situation. Moreover, Nobara's children can be seen as an intervention strategy in the contact zone between herself and the soldiers. As Nobara could speak English and was well versed in government regulations, she could earn over 15,000 yen a month or more through sex work with numerous Occupation soldiers. This monthly income is about three times higher than the US$20 (5,400 yen) monthly income of a soldier mentioned in the introduction to this book. Rather than hiding her children from the soldiers because they were Japanese, Nobara could appeal to the soldiers to provide them with gifts as a part of her survival strategy, as a kind of armor.

Chapter

4

Survival Strategies
in Love

An overwhelming majority of the sixty-three accounts selected for analysis from the *Streetwalkers* publication describe a love affair with an Occupation soldier. Love affairs between such soldiers and women in occupied territories were decidedly asymmetric relationships. For this reason, in this chapter, I discuss the survival strategies used by Japanese women in their intimate relationships with Occupation soldiers.

According to Mühlhäuser, some soldiers created 'similar worlds' in occupied territories – worlds akin to, but clearly separated from, their lives at home. She cites an example given by Jewish survivor Sheli Lagin of a German cook with a wife and two children in Germany, and a second 'wife' in occupied Lithuania, whose two lives never crossed paths (Mühlhäuser 2020: 198).

There were similar cases of Occupation soldiers who created pseudo-marriages in occupied Japan that were distinct from their lives at home.

The women listed in category A of Table 4.1 were those in occupied territories who lived with soldiers in a pseudo-marriage. Those listed in categories B to D had soldiers visit them in their rooms. Women in category B continued to work in some capacity, while those listed in category C were unemployed and lived on a monthly allowance from an Occupation soldier. Those in category D were women whose partners introduced them to a friend (another soldier) before returning home. Occupations followed by '(present)' are those that women worked in at the time they were interviewed. The assets that women possessed when they encountered an Occupation soldier have been divided into educational background, money, connections and beauty. An educated background shows that a woman had cultural resources; money suggests that her family had economic resources; connections are an indicator of social resources;

and beauty is an asset all on its own. Regarding the latter, I classified a woman as beautiful if her former occupation was one that tended to involve good looks, such as actress, dancer and the like. As mentioned earlier, dancers were not stage dancers, but women who were assigned to Occupation soldiers as dance partners.[1]

Table 4.1 shows that many women were former dancers, suggesting that Occupation soldiers who did not intend to marry women from occupied territories chose partners largely based on their looks. The pseudo-marriages that these couples entered into were 'marriages' limited in place to occupied territories and in time to the soldier's deployment. Soldiers were therefore less concerned with their partner's educational background, financial status or connections. Indeed, because relationships were so clearly limited to occupied territories, money or connections held by the woman or her family would probably have been a hindrance.

The monthly allowances that Occupation soldiers gave their partners varied. Women listed in category A of Table 4.1 who lived with soldiers had sizeable monthly incomes and lived in areas with residential and other facilities for officers. By contrast, Aki, Natsuko and Nanoka received less than 10,000 yen. Aki's partner was a soldier, as I will discuss later. Satsuki graduated from a girls' high school before becoming a dancer at a cabaret, where she met a black soldier. That she boarded with him in Fushimi ward suggests that Fushimi ward was an area where black soldiers lived.

The Mokuren whom I discussed in Chapter 2 is the same Mokuren listed in category B. After she was sexually assaulted, a woman raped by Occupation soldiers alongside her introduced her to a cabaret in Otsu, where Mokuren began working. At this cabaret, Mokuren met an Occupation soldier by the name of 'J' who 'looked rich, since he rode around

Table 4.1 Features of women in occupied territories that actively

	Name	Age	Educational background	Money	Connections	Beauty
A	Kanon	20	Public girls' high school		✓	
	Ran	27	Girls' vocational school		✓	✓
	Karin	25	Girls' high school	✓	✓	✓
	Yukiko	19	Elementary school			
	Tsubaki	19	Elementary school			✓
	Iris	Unknown	Unknown			
B	Kaede	21	Unknown	✓	✓	✓
	Rin	34	Girls' high school			✓
	Mokuren	20	Girls' vocational school		✓	✓
C	Aki	17	Elementary school			
	Asa	19	Girls' high school	✓	✓	
	Satsuki	22	Girls' high school		✓	✓
	Natsuko	20	Girls' commercial school			✓
	Nanoka	21	Elementary school			
D	Akiko	22	Unknown			✓
	Yuzu	20	Girls' high school	✓		✓

Notes: Religion, though not examined, was also a factor.
A = Women in occupied territories who lived with soldiers in a pseudo-marriage.
B = Women who also worked in some capacity.

on a motorcycle and had his own taxi'. Though they were intimate, J had no qualms about returning home in March 1948. Mokuren only knew he was leaving when she saw him on a departure truck from a distance.

Meanwhile, Ran (aged twenty-seven) 'enjoyed' living with a thirty-year-old senior officer, but was forced to leave when the officer's wife arrived, suggesting that officers who were married (and possibly had children) dated women from occupied territories as temporary substitutes until their wives relocated to Japan.

contributed to them falling in love with Occupation soldiers

Monthly income (yen)	Former occupation	Address
Unknown (her partner was a high-ranking officer)	Employee of E Bureau, Kobe City	Sakyo ward
20,000	Office worker at N Wool	Sakyo ward
Forced to give up a 20,000 salary to live with her partner	Club worker	Kamigyo ward
30,000	Wartime employee of N Batteries → dressmaker	Higashiku-jyo
30,000	Unemployed	Sakyo ward
Unknown	Teacher	Sakyo ward
15,000	Daiei Film actress → PX worker (present)	Sakyo ward
10,000	Dancer and café worker (present)	Sakyo ward
45,000	Dancer (present)	Kyoto
7,000 to 8,000	Side job dyeing cloth for *obiage*	Fushimi ward
30,000 to 40,000	Red Cross hospital nurse	Sakyo ward
10,000 (black soldier)	Dancer	Fushimi ward
6,000	Cabaret	Shi-jyo
5 every two months + dresses, jewellery, food	Movie theater	Sakyo ward
As much as needed in Japanese currency	Dancer (present)	Higashiyama ward
25,000	Elevator girl	Sakyo ward

C = Women who were unemployed and lived on a monthly allowance from an occupying soldier.

D = Women whose partners introduced them to a friend (another soldier) before returning home.

Like Ran, Karin (aged twenty-five) also lived with an Occupation soldier, but her partner returned home after they had lived together for a year. Before meeting her partner, Karin worked at a club and earned 20,000 yen per month but quit after her partner urged her to do so. To her partner, it must have seemed as though he had succeeded in 'capturing' the popular Karin and turning her into his 'local wife'. Karin's family wealth, as well as Ran's educational and employment history (she graduated from a girls' vocational school and was a secretary at a well-established wool company in

Kobe before the war), suggest that Occupation soldiers who were ranked as officers or higher sought women from corresponding social classes as their 'local wives'.

When Yukiko (aged nineteen), the eldest daughter of a shoemaker, was mistakenly rounded up with women in relationships with soldiers and taken to a hospital for VD testing, she 'saw everyone wearing beautiful clothes and make-up'. She had a dressmaker friend of hers take her to a party, where Yukiko fell in love with a soldier who was a 'cook'. She lived with him on the second floor of a boarding house in Fushimi, and when she became pregnant, her partner initially asked her to keep the baby. However, when the soldier learned that he would be returning home, he urged Yukiko to have an abortion. The soldier returned home one week after Yukiko had the procedure, three months after she had moved in with him. The cook never proposed to Yukiko.

The stories of Mokuren, Ran, Karin and Yukiko are typical examples of the asymmetric romantic relationships between Occupation soldiers and women in occupied territories. These romances, limited as they were to the occupied territories, were useful for the soldiers. Yet if we examine them using the concept of the contact zone, we can see how such relationships illustrate the ways in which Japanese women used their agency to their advantage to strategically become the exclusive sweethearts of Occupation soldiers.

Women who captivated Occupation soldiers

Asa, who made her soldier extend his stay when he was ordered to repatriate

During World War II, Asa (aged nineteen) dropped out of a Kyoto girls' high school after two years and volunteered as a nurse at a hospital for injured veterans in Osaka. Both of her brothers were then in the army. After working at a nurses' training school for three years, Asa worked for three months at Osaka Second Red Cross Hospital. The war escalated, and she was dispatched to the Red Cross Hospital in Pyongyang (Korea), from which she returned with twenty-five to twenty-six other nurses at the end of the war. Asa later grew close to an Occupation soldier who worked as a photographic developer, whom she met through her uncle, who had returned to Kyoto from the US. The soldier promised to marry her, but permission from the US only arrived after his return to his home country, and they were never married.[2] Asa later began an exclusive intimate relationship with a different soldier. At the time of her interview, their relationship was ongoing. It is highly likely that this soldier was an officer, judging by his request to delay his return to the US by three years, and the sizeable sum of 30,000 to 40,000 yen that he gave Asa each month. Asa's previous partner, who gave Asa 3,000 yen per month, was probably a low-ranking soldier who lacked the capacity to apply to extend his stay.

Asa specified neither where nor how she had met the soldier who applied to extend his stay. She did, however, note that her uncle was visited by many soldiers, suggesting that his job was important to the occupying forces. It is therefore possible that she also met the second soldier through her uncle's job. Furthermore, if we note how Asa herself used 'income' to refer to the money she received from her second partner, we can see that while the soldier loved Asa to the extent of applying to stay in Japan, Asa saw the relationship as a means of earning a living. This was Asa's survival strategy.

Iris, the older former schoolteacher who continued to live with an Occupation soldier

When Kazu was an elementary school student, Iris (a pseudonym) was one of the women who was particularly kind to her. Iris lived near Kazu's house with a soldier called Noam. Kazu loved women who were beautiful and stylish, and her impression of Iris was that she was over forty and unfashionable. Kazu's mother was then in her late thirties, and Iris looked even older. 'As a child, I couldn't understand how Mr. Noam could love an older woman with a twitching face'.

Noam himself was an older soldier, and he and Iris got along well, calling each other by their given names. Iris was a schoolteacher before the war, and she tutored Kazu during her frequent visits. Her speech, according to Kazu, was 'by the book', suggesting that she might have been from the Tokyo area. At the very least, she was presumably not from Kyoto. When Kazu visited them, she saw a photograph of MacArthur pinned to the wall, showing the general at the airport. Noam was also in the picture. When Kazu told her father, he said, 'Mr. Noam's actually a pretty important guy'. Noam was probably an officer, judging from both his photograph with MacArthur and the fact that he was living with Iris.

Kazu remembers sleeping at the home of Noam and Iris. In another fond memory, she recalls learning English from them. Noam and Iris were happy together, but never married. According to Kazu, 'One day, she [Iris] told me that Mr. Noam had a family in America, and a child about my age'. Perhaps Noam identified Kazu and Iris with the child and wife he had left in the US. Noam continued living with Iris in Kyoto until he was deployed to the Korean War. That he continued to live with Iris while in occupied Japan shows that he loved her.

Though Iris was educated, she was neither young nor attractive. Noam's interest in her could therefore be attributed to Iris being 'a woman you could date comfortably, who didn't pester you about marriage'. There, however, no need for a soldier of Noam's status to be so devoted to Iris. It would have been entirely possible for him to find a young, highly educated woman. This is because women who sought close relationships with Occupation soldiers craved exclusivity. Yet Noam stayed true to Iris until he had to leave Japan for the Korean War. If we examine their relationship using the concept of the contact zone, we can see that Iris held Noam's heart until he left Japan. This was Iris's survival strategy.

Nanoka, who captivated an Occupation soldier and a hospital director

Nanoka (aged twenty-one) dropped out of elementary school after completing the fourth grade and lived with her mother and five siblings as a family of seven. While working at a 'Western movie theater' she began seeing an Occupation soldier (age unknown). They did not live together. While dating, Nanoka was caught by the military police (MP) and hospitalized with a VD. While she was in hospital, the soldier she was dating visited her daily. He brought her 'Chocs, cigs, butter, bread and food'. Nanoka spent three months in the hospital. The soldier returned home during her second month there, and Nanoka received the hospital director's permission to see him off at the station.

According to Nanoka's account, the soldier was devoted to her, at least while he was stationed in Japan. He certainly visited her almost daily while she was in the hospital. During this time, they could not have sex. If he had only been after her body, the soldier could have ended their relationship when Nanoka was hospitalized and found another woman, but he chose not to. Even if he did not break up with her, if sex had been his main objective, he could have visited a 'whorehouse' while Nanoka was hospitalized. Yet this soldier visited her in the hospital every day until his departure. Before she was hospitalized, the soldier gave her dresses, shoes and makeup, but only five yen once every two months. In modern terms, this would have amounted to 500 yen. That he only gave her such a small amount once every two months suggests that Nanoka's partner was probably a private, yet that would have been meagre even for a private, so he may have been sending most of his salary to a family back in the US.

We should also note the fact that Nanoka was able to receive the hospital director's permission to farewell her partner when he returned to the US. This is significant, as it shows that she was able to enlist the support not just of a hospital staff member, but of someone who worked there in a managerial role. As I discuss in detail in my book *Panpan to wa dare nano ka* (hereafter, *Who Were Panpan?*), at the time, hospitals for VDs were explicitly designed to prevent infected women from escaping. They were closely monitored, with barbed-wire fences, barred windows and security guards posted at entrances. Under these circumstances, there was no way that Nanoka, still not fully recovered, would have been allowed to farewell her soldier. Those who 'escaped' the hospital were lynched. The implication here is that not only did Nanoka captivate an Occupation soldier, but she also drew the attention of the hospital director. Nanoka came from a lower socioeconomic class and was poorly educated, having dropped out of elementary school in the fourth grade. Her interview responses were written in simple sentences, using *hiragana*, and interviewers frequently had to substitute *kanji* for her expressions.[3] Different as they were, both the soldier and the hospital director were persons of authority, yet they ultimately bent to the will of the relatively powerless Nanoka.

Nanoka's example shows how women in occupied territories who were the weaker parties in asymmetric power relationships could assert themselves. Even women from lower socioeconomic backgrounds, far from positions of power, could behave in ways that allowed them to shape the circumstances in which they found themselves.

Women who frustrated the aims of Occupation soldiers

Hana, who refused to let a soldier take her child

The case of Hana (aged twenty-one) is not included in Table 4.1. This is because, as I shall discuss further, Hana and her partner did not meet in Kyoto. Hana became romantically involved with an Occupation soldier whom she met in her hometown, in Kumamoto. However, the soldier was transferred to Kyoto without Hana's knowledge, and immediately returned home from there. The child born to Hana and the soldier was 'a cute child, with [REDACTED] eyes'. This probably refers to the child's eye color, which was possibly blue or green. That the child's eye color was censored doubtless indicates that their father was a white soldier.

Hana, born in November 1927, began dating an Occupation soldier when she was eighteen, and bore his child when she was about nineteen. When her child's father was transferred to Kyoto, Hana left her child in the care of her mother and followed the soldier to Kyoto. He had, however, already returned home.

While still in Kumamoto, the soldier had given Hana 1,200 yen to cover the admission fee when their child fell ill and needed to be hospitalized. This suggests that the soldier knew that Hana had given birth to his child. Yet he still went to Kyoto without telling her, and returned home from there, suggesting that he saw his relationship with Hana as one that was clearly limited to occupied Japan. According to Hana's account, the soldier never recognized the child as his own.

Hana remained in Kyoto and engaged in sex work with unspecified US soldiers to earn a living. She had a monthly income of over 10,000 yen, of which she sent 3,000 to 4,000 yen back to her child in Kumamoto. Hana averaged one or two US soldiers per day and was paid an advance of 600 to 700 (and sometimes as much as 1,000) yen by each client.

Hana lived in Fukakusa, near an Occupation force camp for privates. This, together with the regularity with which she saw multiple clients each day, suggests that Hana's clients were not officers. If Hana were picking up officers who lived in the Okazaki area, she would have had to have lived near Okazaki to find multiple clients each day. It would have taken too long to travel from Fukakusa to Okazaki.

While Hana was working for clients in Kyoto, her child's father sent an intermediary to bring the child to the US. The soldier's primary concern was his biological child, and not Hana. Yet events did not proceed as the soldier had planned. Hana plainly rejected the soldier's offer and also rejected a French church that sought custody of her child. This case that involved a religious institution seeking custody of Hana's child echoes research conducted by the historian Takuya Onodera, who notes, with reference to children born to German soldiers and local women during World War II, that 'there was a move to acquire "racially desirable" children, who were registered, screened, and taken to Germany to become part of the "Deutsche Volksgemeinschaft [German national community]"' (Onodera 2017: 37). Would the French church have wanted Hana's child if the child had not been white? For that matter, could it be that Hana's mother in Kumamoto took care of Hana's child because the child was 'a cute child, with [REDACTED] eyes'?

To the Occupation soldier who welcomed an asymmetric relationship with a woman from occupied Japan and then returned home to the US, Hana's refusal to grant him custody of their child was doubtless a shock. Asymmetric though their relationship may have been, by refusing to hand over her child, Hana ultimately defied the soldier's intentions.

Yuko, who took the sexual initiative

Seventeen-year-old Yuko was raised as the adopted daughter of her father's younger brother and his wife. She dropped out of a girls' commercial school in her second year and learned dressmaking while helping her stepmother. Of Yuko's older biological sisters, the eldest graduated from a girls' teacher training school and became an elementary school teacher, while the younger was a dressmaker who also helped with the housework, suggesting that Yuko's biological family was relatively wealthy. It is likely that Yuko was adopted by her father's younger brother and his wife not for financial reasons, but perhaps because the younger couple could not have children.

Yuko went to Kyoto's Keihan Sanjo, hoping to get help from a schoolfriend, and started a relationship with 'B', a nineteen-year-old Occupation soldier whom she met at the home of a woman she had met at the train station. Before they were introduced, Yuko had said 'I want someone meek, like a Japanese person', so B was probably 'someone meek'. B was Yuko's first time. He gave her 2,000 yen, and brought her a box of chocolates, three cans of sardines and a box of crackers the next day. Thereafter, Yuko lived in 'an aunty's *panpan* house' near Keihan Sanjo, while continuing to meet B at a separate location.

Yuko was a resourceful woman. As she could not speak English, she took English conversation classes for about a month, without telling her stepmother. Yuko's hometown, where she had learned dressmaking while helping with the housework, was surrounded by fields and did not even have a movie theater. Yuko therefore told her stepmother that she had learned English and wanted to live independently in Kyoto, where she could use her English to work at a photography studio. Her stepmother objected, but Yuko finally convinced her and moved to Kyoto.

It was this very resourcefulness that enabled Yuko to clearly express her preference for 'someone meek' before being introduced to an Occupation soldier. Yuko's partner apparently visited her every day and tried to satiate his 'physical needs' twice a week. When Yuko was particularly tired, she would refuse to gratify him, saying 'I'm really tired today'. An additional note by Yuko's interviewer claims that she was of 'below average intelligence'. In a previous work, I argued that this judgement potentially stemmed from Yuko toying with the interviewer (Chazono 2014). This impression was reinforced while preparing this work. Yuko avoided compulsory VD testing and hospitalization by moving from one friend's house to another, and by meeting B at a separate location; in short, she was not only resourceful, but also quite bright. This suggests that she might have deliberately downplayed her intelligence, leading the interviewer to note that she had 'below average intelligence'. Not only did Yuko take the sexual initiative in her relationship with a soldier, she was also able to outwit her interviewer. This was Yuko's survival strategy.

Women who did not rely on Occupation soldiers

Women in German-occupied territories who were involved with German soldiers were subject to sudden changes, such as the deployment of their partners. 'The women were forming relationships with men whose near future was completely uncertain' (Mühlhäuser 2020: 203). The situation was the same for Japanese women who were intimately involved with Occupation soldiers.

I used the example of Karin at the start of this chapter as an example of how Occupation soldiers who sought 'local wives' had local women leave their jobs to live with them. On the other hand, there were soldiers who did not ask their partners to stop working, even when their jobs as dancers required them to dance one-on-one with unspecified soldiers. It is possible that these soldiers were dating multiple women.

If we examine the asymmetric romantic relationships in occupied Japan using the concept of the contact zone, we can see how some women did not rely on Occupation soldiers. By not relying on soldiers, they avoided experiences that were 'just as unpleasant or even as frightening as the prospect of suddenly being alone again' (Mühlhäuser 2020: 203). I will now discuss two such cases.

Kaede, a cabaret worker and former actress

Kaede (aged twenty-one), a former actress, was born in Nagoya, and was living in Sakyo ward at the time of her interview. Her parents' relationship was strained, and her father left when Kaede was five years old. While she was an actress, Kaede met an Occupation soldier in Kyoto's red-light district when visiting one of her mother's friends who worked as a manager there. Kaede quit acting in October 1946, one month after the soldier returned home. They had met soon after the Occupation forces arrived in Kyoto, implying that Kaede was still an actress while she was dating the soldier.

Kaede became involved in the relationship because she 'wanted money'.

> I entered a film production company, Daiei, wanting to be a star, but I realized that dating Japanese men and taking their money might cause trouble later. If they were [REDACTED], they'd [REDACTED], and in the end I thought I'd feel safer, so I dated them. My mom knew a lot about what I was doing, and she gave me approval and advice.

Kaede dated Occupation soldiers and took their money, with her mother's consent. She avoided Japanese men, as this could have negatively impacted her acting career. Kaede was also fully aware that she was in these relationships for money. After Kaede's first partner returned home, she swiftly moved on; at the time of her interview, she was dating her sixth soldier, while simultaneously working at a cabaret in Higashiyama.

According to Kaede, 'I knew the true conditions under which [REDACTED] dated Japanese women, so I dated them flexibly, in a bunesslike [sic] fashion'. This gives us some idea as to how Occupation soldiers saw women in occupied territories. Kaede further stated that, 'I liked them, but I didn't really love them', and 'In this kind of world, if you can live happily with someone, that's just a lus [sic; "plus"]. There's no need to get all serious about it'. These statements suggest that even though Kaede appeared to date one soldier at a time, to her, they were ultimately just a means of obtaining money. She also worked at a cabaret because she well knew that the soldiers could be sent home at any time. Kaede was a woman who was not prepared to be financially dependent on Occupation soldiers.

Rin, who juggled work at a dance hall and a café

Rin (aged thirty-four) dropped out of a girls' high school in Okinawa after two years and went to Yokohama, where her parents were working. At the age of about twenty-one, she married and had a son. After her divorce, Rin left her son in the care of her ex-husband, and went to her mother in Osaka, where she supported her mother by working as a dancer in Otsu. A dancer's monthly income was 3,000 yen at the time, of which Rin gave 2,000 to 2,500 yen to her mother. While working as a dancer, she started exclusively dating an Occupation soldier she met at the dance hall. Rin did not say when their relationship began, but the soldier returned home on 3 January 1949. After his departure, Rin moved to Kyoto and lived with a different soldier, with whom she was in an exclusive relationship, while working at both a dance hall and a café.

Of the sixty-three women who featured in *Streetwalkers* selected for analysis in this book, it is worth noting that Rin was the second oldest, after thirty-six-year-old Nobara. Most women who dated soldiers were around twenty years of age. Specifically, sixty-eight percent of women were between nineteen and twenty-four years of age. Only eight percent of women were over thirty. This eight percent includes women who were renting rooms to sex workers.

Former nurse Rira (aged twenty-three) was much younger than Rin. After hearing many stories from *panpan* at the hospital, she thought 'this is it', and quit nursing to engage in sex work with Occupation soldiers. She started by exclusively dating a soldier who gave her 20,000 yen per month, but when he returned home, she began dating multiple soldiers. Rira was dating many soldiers in her search for monogamy: 'I just want to be with one [REDACTED], that's who I'm looking for'. She earned 5,000 to 8,000 yen per month.

It is worth noting that Rin, who was more than eleven years older than Rira, was soon in a monogamous relationship with a different soldier after her first partner returned home. Not only did Rin's income from her partner surpass Rira's at 10,000 yen per month, but in addition to continuing the relationship, Rin also worked at a dance hall and a café. This shows that Rin did not become solely dependent on her relationship. Even if her relationship with the Occupation solider were to end suddenly, Rin had ensured that she would be able to support herself. This was Rin's survival strategy.

Women who sought monogamous relationships as a survival strategy

Women who were in exclusive relationships with Occupation soldiers in occupied territories were afforded the wealth and power of the victor. This of course meant that some women in these territories coveted monogamous relationships with soldiers. These women were infamously labelled 'Western whores'. This section discusses women who made strategic use of monogamous relationships.

Aki, who laid thorough groundwork for an exclusive relationship

'It's heaven as long as I don't get rounded up'. So said Aki (aged seventeen), an elementary school graduate who lived with her mother and one of five older sisters, regarding her life as the exclusive partner of an Occupation soldier. Her father had left her mother fifteen years prior and moved in with his 'mistress' in a different prefecture. She also had an older brother who had already left home. Aki married a city hall worker in February 1948, but her husband's extravagant lifestyle drove her back to her home in Kyoto, where she earned a living through a side job dyeing cloth for *obiage* (scarf-like pieces of long cloth used to hold *obi* in place, or as accessories). Still struggling to make ends meet, Aki slept with a soldier she met through a friend, and he gave her '300 yen, a box of chocolates, beer and canned food'. Afterward, according to Aki, 'I became desperate, I wanted to be in a relationship with [REDACTED], and I learned English and rented a room'. In short, Aki made preparations before meeting a soldier through a friend and becoming his exclusive partner.

It was only after she first slept with an Occupation soldier for money that Aki learned that being in an exclusive relationship with a soldier made it easier to receive money and gifts regularly. As exclusivity guaranteed a stable monthly income and lifestyle, there was fierce competition among women in occupied territories who desired such relationships with Occupation soldiers. Aki's decision to learn English suggests that she was looking for an educated soldier. She needed 'polite English' that was not 'Panglish' (the one-word English spoken by *panpan*). According to Kazu, some of the Occupation soldiers she met when she was in elementary school could not read or write. So, Kazu's father, who was a university graduate and spoke some English, would write letters in English for such soldiers. There was no guarantee of the financial stability of soldiers who needed to ask for assistance with writing. This is because the difference in education was tied to the soldiers' rank. Only by becoming an officer's partner could one be assured of a prosperous life. For Aki, who lacked education, money and connections, being thoroughly well-prepared was her survival strategy. By learning English and renting a room in advance, she was able to become the exclusive partner of an Occupation soldier.

Kanon, who chose monogamy due to poverty and her fascination with Occupation soldiers

Kanon (aged twenty) graduated from a public girls' high school in Kobe, Hyogo prefecture, before working for the city. She and her eight-year-old brother had lost both their parents in the bombing of Kobe. Kanon's father had run a confectionary business, which would have made Kanon the daughter of a company director. That she was able to work for Kobe City also suggests that she was well-connected with people from her high school. Though her salary was 100 yen per month, including meals, she was only paid once every three months. Struggling with poverty, Kanon left her brother in the care of her mother's friend and moved to Osaka, where she earned a living as a maid on the black market.

While working as a kitchen maid, Kanon met a friend. At the time, her friend was engaged in sex work with Occupation soldiers in a room that she rented at a *ryokan* (Japanese inn). Kanon, who was 'also fascinated with [REDACTED], and desperately struggling to get by', met a soldier through one of her friend's clients. 'The [REDACTED] was the head of [RECACTED]. He was high-ranking at [RECACTED]'. The person in question could possibly have worked at GHQ. Kanon lived with him in his rooms for six months, until he returned home. Though Kanon herself never described her partner beyond 'He was high-ranking at [REDACTED]', he was probably a high-ranking officer. There were rules dictating that privates return to camp, and there were living quarters set aside specifically for unmarried officers. Either option would have made it difficult for the soldier to live with Kanon.

Kanon met this soldier through the intimate partner of one of her friends. After her first partner returned home, Kanon began exclusively dating a different Occupation soldier, whom she was seeing at the time of her interview. This, together with how Kanon was able to be in a monogamous relationship with a high-ranking officer, strongly suggests that Kanon's friend was also involved with an officer. In other words, both Kanon and Kanon's friend were probably from a higher socioeconomic class. Kanon used her circumstances to actively encourage her friend to introduce her to an Occupation soldier. Kanon's survival strategy was not to find just any soldier, but one that met her expectations. This led to her being in an exclusive relationship with a high-ranking officer, and that was her survival strategy.

Natsuko, driven by conflict with her adoptive parents and wanting to make it on her own as an 'only'

'I think it's closed-minded of people to straightaway assume relationships with [REDACTED] are bad. I don't think there's anything wrong with loving a [REDACTED]'. Twenty-year-old Natsuko's objections to society's critical view of romantic relationships with Occupation soldiers shows that she thought of herself not as a mistress, but as a lover. Natsuko was a graduate of a girls' commercial school, and her adoptive parents were supported by Natsuko's stepsister and her husband. Differences of opinion between Natsuko and her adoptive parents prompted her to move out and live independently. While living at home, Natsuko had worked a little as a dressmaker, but after she moved out, she worked at a local dance school, earning 500 yen per month. She later moved to Kyoto and worked at a dance hall, before living and working at a cabaret in Otsu. It was there that she began seeing a soldier.

At the time of her interview with the Kyoto Social Welfare Research Center, Natsuko was in a relationship with a twenty-two-year-old soldier. Natsuko's partner spent the weekends with her at her place in Shijo-Matsubara, but would leave at around 9pm. As he lacked the freedom to stay out, the soldier was probably a private. According to Natsuko, 'He brings me all sorts of sweets, like chewing gum, chocolate and candy, and we drink beer, dance and have fun. We go to the skating rink in Sanjo, see movies at Asahi Kaikan, go to the [REDACTED] Club, that sort of thing'. Furthermore, 'My monthly income is about 6,000 yen. [NAME REDACTED] gets me what I need. I get a pack of cigarettes a day, beer to drink and magazines like "*Style*" and "*Bibo* [Beauty]"'. Natsuko's words suggest that she was enjoying her relationship with the soldier: 'I'm enjoying my current lifestyle, and I don't feel like going home'.

Natsuko adds, however, that 'If my parents told me to come home, I would'. The implication that she would be willing to return home if her adoptive parents' attitude changed suggests that, for Natsuko, her relationship was a means of distancing herself from her adoptive parents and the difficult relationship she had with them. Though prepared to return home if her parents asked her to, Natsuko, like Aki and Kanon, used a relationship with an Occupation soldier to be independent. Leaving her parents and enjoying American culture was Natsuko's survival strategy.

Survival strategies that used homosociality

When Occupation soldiers were due to return home, some introduced the women they had been seeing in occupied territories to their friends. This was done partly to ensure that the women continued to be supported financially. However, it is important to note that this concern was not entirely altruistic as it was also tied to sexual favors linked to homosociality. The introduction of a sexual partner to a friend was part of the homosocial relationship between the returning soldier and his friend. The examples of Akiko and Yuzu, discussed below, both involve using homosocial relationships as a survival strategy.

Akiko, who was intimately involved with a soldier thirty-six years older than her

Akiko (aged twenty-two) was born to a Korean mother and Japanese father, who had died when Akiko was eight years old. When she was around thirteen or fourteen years old, she worked as a salesgirl at a department store in Mukden, Manchuria. While working as a salesgirl, Akiko became involved with J, the son of a tea shop owner in Uji, Kyoto.

When J returned to Kyoto, Akiko went with him. She earned a living working at a factory and lived in an apartment run by J's aunt (his mother's younger sister). As J was adopted by another family, he and Akiko could not be married, and a devastated Akiko began working as a dancer at a dance hall, doubtless driven by her broken heart. It was at this dance hall that Akiko met an Occupation soldier.

> I met [NAME REDACTED] at a dance hall in Higashiyama, and we grew close, but he went home after about a year and a half. He introduced me to my current [REDACTED].

> [NAME REDACTED] is about fifty-eight and I've been seeing
> him exclusively.

The age of Akiko's first partner is unclear, but for him to
have introduced Akiko to a fifty-eight-year-old colleague, the
two must have been officers. Furthermore, the two met in a
dance hall in Higashiyama. The dance hall was probably used
exclusively by officers after the war, as 'it was a high-end
dance hall located halfway up Mt. Kujo [Kujoyama], between
the Miyako Hotel and Yamashina. The wealthy Sannosuke
Amasaki built it at a cost of over one million yen' (Aoki 2013:
308; Sawa, Naramoto and Yoshida, eds., 1984: 764). If Akiko's
first partner frequented this dance hall, both he and Akiko's
second partner must have been officers.

We know nothing about Akiko's background, not even her
educational history. She probably had connections of some
kind through her late father, however, as suggested by her job
as a salesgirl in a Japanese colony, her living in an apartment
complex managed by J's aunt, and her job at a dance hall
that was frequented by officers. Regarding the relationship
between Akiko's parents, if we consider that Akiko's Korean
mother married a Japanese soldier while Korea was under
Japanese rule, we can think of their relationship as mirroring
that of an Occupation soldier and a woman in an occupied
territory. As we have already seen, for an Occupation soldier to
have considered marrying a woman in an occupied territory,
the woman's family would likely have had to have been
wealthy or well-connected. Such conditions would also have
applied to Akiko's parents' marriage. In other words, Akiko's
mother was probably a woman from a higher socioeconomic
class. This would have contributed to the fact that J's aunt
offered Akiko a place to live.

The officer with whom Akiko was involved was old enough to be her father, making it highly likely that he had a wife and child(ren) at home. From this perspective, we can see that by introducing her to a friend when he returned home, he was treating Akiko almost like a pet cat or dog. Perhaps he felt sorry at the thought of abandoning a pet that he had looked after and determined to at least leave her in the care of a friend. As we have seen, when Occupation soldiers were ordered to return home, they did so swiftly, even more so if they had a wife (and/or child) waiting for them.

Nevertheless, Akiko's partner was unable to stand the idea of abandoning Akiko and returning home. Or rather, Akiko's behavior caused the officer to feel this way. That was what drove him to introduce Akiko to a friend of his, resulting in Akiko's relationship with the fifty-eight-year-old soldier. This was Akiko's survival strategy.

Yuzu, who had her eye on marriage as a survival strategy

Yuzu (aged twenty), a graduate of a girls' high school, had met a twenty-seven-year-old Occupation soldier 'with a wife at home' at a hotel when she was eighteen. Hotels were used to house officers living alone, making Yuzu's partner an officer. They had been seeing each other for less than a year when the soldier returned home. As with Akiko's partner, this soldier introduced Yuzu to a different soldier when he was repatriated.

Yuzu's family got by on the income from a coffee shop, and though they were not exactly prosperous, they had enough money to send Yuzu to a girls' high school. Until her parents grew ill and passed away in 1945 and 1946, Yuzu helped at home and did not have to work elsewhere. It is therefore likely that Yuzu's notion of 'just getting by' was very much subjective.

Yuzu specified neither where nor how she met the officer, but she did mention that she was able to work as an elevator girl when they were dating. Given that Yuzu had no parents, it is probable that she secured her job as an elevator girl through her partner. That the officer found her a job as an elevator girl also suggests that she was attractive. Whatever the case, Yuzu's partner was a well-connected officer.

When Yuzu's partner was to return home, he introduced her to a different soldier. The soldier's age is unknown, but as he gave Yuzu 25,000 yen per month, he was probably also an officer. Yuzu purchased a house in Osaka for 250,000 yen by evenly splitting the cost with her partner. When Yuzu's partner moved to Otsu, the house in Osaka was rented out to Yuzu's friends for 1,000 yen per month per person. Unlike her friends, Yuzu was the main registrant on the family register, and she therefore received food rations and other essentials. Yuzu sent her two younger brothers 5,000 yen per month and was able to buy them everything they needed. This all suggests that Yuzu was living comfortably.

Regarding dating an Occupation soldier, Yuzu firmly stated, 'I want to get married if that's possible, but I'm happy with my current lifestyle'. On the other hand, she also said, 'I get anxious when I think about what will happen when [NAME REDACTED] leaves'. Though Yuzu also claimed, 'If I were to work, I'd like a job where I used English', as we have seen, she got her current job through her partner, who also introduced her to someone else when he returned home. Evenly split or not, she was also able to purchase real estate through her partner. Yuzu was able to further improve her lifestyle when she began renting her home to friends for 1,000 yen per month per person after her partner was transferred.

This added layer of financial security was part of Yuzu's survival strategy.

Chapter 5

Marriage as a Survival Strategy

This chapter examines the way women in occupied Japan sought marriage with an Occupation soldier as a survival strategy. Table 5.1 sums up the characteristics of eleven women who were proposed to by Occupation soldiers.

The women's educational background, financial status and social connections are interrelated. All have ties with parents, relatives and other people such as school officials. Those in group A involve cases where the couple received approval for their marriage from the soldier's parents or the woman's parents, while those in group B consist of cases where approval was not received from either set of parents, but the soldier promised to marry the woman anyway. The women receiving large sums of money – e.g., 20,000 to 50,000 yen – from an Occupation soldier were clearly in a relationship with a commissioned officer. These women came from the well-to-do ranks of society, and none of the betrothed soldiers in this survey were involved with a woman from a lower class. Asa (nineteen) and Yuri (twenty) both came from a socioeconomic class higher than those of the soldiers who promised to marry them.

As described in Chapter 4, Asa persuaded the soldier she was dating to apply for an extension to his posting; the soldier she had previously been dating had returned home just before the marriage permit reached her. She came from a well-off family, and her uncle had influential contacts at GHQ, because his workplace was a location where many Occupation soldiers gathered. Asa was so in love with one of the soldiers that they submitted a marriage application. The fact that this was approved reveals the strength of her uncle's ties with the Occupation forces. From Asa's narrative it is clear that economic capital (her family was affluent) and social capital (her uncle had connections, and Asa's previous job was as a Red Cross nurse) were important elements in becoming the legal spouse of an Occupation soldier. Moreover, the reason that Asa did not complete girls' high school was so that she could become a nurse. The fact that her fiancé returned home while the marriage application was still pending suggests that he was not entitled to extend his stay in Japan while awaiting the outcome of the application. This reveals a gap between the soldier's status and Asa's social standing.

Yuri came from an affluent family, and both her parents were alive and well at the time of her participation in the survey. She graduated from a girls' high school and ran a dressmaking shop, and she had a seventeen-year-old younger brother. When she herself was seventeen, Yuri met an Occupation soldier (aged twenty-six at that time) and lost her virginity to him. They were still in love, and Yuri said she wanted to marry him. Since this soldier drove cars for a living back home, Yuri clearly had a higher social standing than him, as was the case with Asa's relationship.

The Occupation soldier to whom Ichigo (twenty-one) was engaged suddenly died, so their marriage could not go ahead. Ichigo's father had worked as a section manager at a company in Kyoto and also as a company president. After Ichigo graduated from girls' high school, she attended a women's college, so she was well educated. Because her father had died five years earlier from a heart attack, Ichigo's family made ends meet through money her maternal grandfather sent them in addition to the wages Ichigo earned after quitting the women's college and becoming a housekeeper to help out with the family finances. She subsequently worked in T Building but was forced to resign after she contracted cardiac beriberi. When Ichigo was nineteen, she had been involved in a relationship with a twenty-year-old Occupation soldier. They had intended to marry, but he suddenly passed away. Although Ichigo stated that she was not involved with

Table 5.1 Characteristics of eleven Japanese women proposed to

Name	Age	Educational background	Financial status	Social connections	Beauty
A[2] Asa	19	Dropped out of girls' high school	✓	✓	
Umeko	21	Dropped out of women's college		✓	
Sakurako	21	Elementary school, then nurses' training school		✓	✓
Shunka	21	Not known	✓	✓	
Tsukushi	18	Girls' high school, then dropped out of Takarazuka Theater	✓	✓	✓
Natsume	19	Dropped out of women's college	✓	✓	✓
B[3] Ichigo	21	Dropped out of women's college	✓	✓	
Tamako	19	Dropped out of girls' high school		✓	✓
Hamana	17	Dropped out of girls' high school	✓	✓	
Fuji	Not known	Graduated girls' high school	✓	✓	
Yuri	20	Graduated girls' high school	✓	✓	

Notes:
1 Here this means the woman is a Christian (Catholic) or has graduated from a Catholic school.
2 Group A consists of cases where the soldier's parents or the woman's parents have given their approval to the marriage.

anyone other than this soldier, her narrative reveals how women like her who were in an intimate relationship with an Occupation soldier were rounded up as *panpan*.

In this way, there was an overwhelming power imbalance between men on the occupying side and women from the occupied nation, even when it came to marriage.

Based on the above, a reexamination of Table 5.1 from the perspective of women's agency in occupied Japan reveals that what these women shared in addition to their well-off background was their ability to elicit a marriage proposal from the soldiers.[1]

by Occupation soldiers

Religion[1]	Monthly income	Previous job	Current address
		Red Cross	Sakyo ward, Kyoto
✓	20,000 yen	Typist for US forces	Sakyo ward, Kyoto
		Waitress on military base	Fushimi ward, Kyoto
	20,000–30,000 yen	Maid	Sakyo ward, Kyoto
✓	30,000–50,000 yen	Typist for US forces	Higashiyama ward, Kyoto
		Actress (traditional Japanese performing arts)	Sakyo ward, Kyoto
✓		Housekeeper	Sakyo ward, Kyoto
		Dancer	Higashiyama ward, Kyoto
		Not employed	Maizuru
	Only received clothes etc.	Runs a dressmaking shop (ongoing)	Sakyo ward, Kyoto
		Runs a dressmaking shop (ongoing)	Fushimi ward, Kyoto

3 Group B consists of cases where parents on neither side have approved of the marriage, but the soldier has promised to marry the woman.

Women proposed to by an Occupation soldier

Shunka: fallback plan if marriage is impossible

Shunka (twenty-one) lost her father when she was four years old. He had owned a box manufacturing business with twenty-three employees. After his death, Shunka was raised by her mother, who rented out rooms for commercial use. Shunka was the youngest in the family, with two older brothers and two older sisters. After graduating from girls' high school she became a housemaid. Shunka's comments – 'My family made a comfortable living from renting out rooms, so it didn't matter how much I earned as a maid'; 'I used my earnings as pocket money' – clearly indicate that her family was well off. While working as a maid, Shunka became involved with an Occupation soldier 'out of curiosity'. She subsequently took a day off work, pretending that a case of roundworms was the reason for her absense.

The soldier Shunka was dating was a wrestler back home, and Shunka was on good terms with his family, exchanging letters with them. She stated that she wanted to marry him one day. He had expressed a strong desire to marry her, suggesting that this would be easier if they had a child together. Shunka lived in a rented house, and he gave her 20,000 to 30,000 yen per month as well as clothing, alcohol and cigarettes, so she says she was comfortably off and did not have to work. She sometimes introduced other girls to newly arrived soldiers. The Occupation soldier provided Shunka with a comfortable life, and he was so captivated by her that he longed to marry her. Shunka made this soldier fall head over heels in love with her in the contact zone that existed between them. She commented that 'We are clearly in a love relationship, and I feel a strong commitment to and sense of authenticity in our life together'.

Nevertheless, Shunka was also highly pragmatic. To start with, she did not inform her mother that the soldier was keen to marry her. The reason for this secrecy was that although Shunka's mother did basically accept the couple's involvement, she was very concerned about their relationship. Secondly, even though the soldier had told Shunka that he wanted to have children with her, she had not expressed her own feelings on the matter. This is evident in her comment that 'If we can't get married, I'd like to run a dressmaking shop, because I've got some savings'. Presumably she had saved up enough to open a dressmaking shop from the money the soldier gave her each month. While enjoying life with the soldier, hoping to marry him, and even corresponding with his family, Shunka was simultaneously formulating a backup plan in case things did not work out.

Although Natsume (nineteen) was also dating an Occupation soldier with a view to marriage and was likewise corresponding with his family back home, it is noteworthy that her thinking differed from that of Shunka. Natsume was from an affluent family and was performing at GHQ's Kyoto Stateside Theater (Kyoto Takarazuka Theater, 1935–45) without her family's knowledge. This theater sometimes put on 'Japanese-style shows' for the families of American commissioned officers (Aoki 2013: 311), presenting traditional Japanese performing arts solely for the enjoyment of commissioned officers and their families. Although it was a classy theater, the fact that Natsume was performing there without her family's knowledge indicates her high-spirited personality. She met the soldier while performing at this theater, soon after which they moved in together. Natsume's strong temperament was the reason she had been proposed to by a soldier who was sufficiently well off to allow them to live together and why she was in touch with his family back home. Natsume had spare time on her hands and wanted employment, but her boyfriend would not hear of it. Even so, she was concerned about whether she would be able to marry him one day, given the 'current international situation'. Unlike Shunka, however, this does not mean that Natsume had a backup plan. Because her family was well off, she probably did not need to formulate such a plan – yet Shunka likewise came from an affluent family.

Although Shunka well and truly won over her soldier and even became involved with his family, she also had the presence of mind to make plans in case they were unable to marry. This cool-headed approach was her survival strategy.

Fuji: drawing parents into the contact zone

Fuji (age unknown), a graduate of a girls' high school, was the daughter of a man with a very healthy income from running a public bathhouse and a fishing brokerage in the countryside. He had both economic and social capital. Fuji came to Kyoto with her two younger sisters, and after studying at a dress-making school for three months she opened a dressmaking shop. Presumably, her father gave her the money to start her business. According to the investigator's note, Fuji studied Urasenke tea ceremony and Ikenobo ikebana (the Japanese art of floral design) for three years and was licensed to teach both, so she was clearly the daughter of a man of considerable means and had cultural capital in the form of her education and accomplishments.

The Occupation soldier (twenty-six years old) Fuji was dating slept at her place every night and hoped to marry her. Fuji's parents had given their approval for this relationship on the condition that the couple marry. Out of all the sixty-three cases from *Streetwalkers* analyzed here, Fuji's is the only case where the woman's parents approved of their daughter's marriage to an Occupation soldier. Moreover, although Fuji did receive items such as clothing from her fiancé, she received no money from him. Because Fuji's wealthy parents approved of the marriage, she had no need for financial assistance from the soldier. What is unusual about Fuji's case is that she brought her parents, who were living under occupation, into the contact zone between herself and the soldier. The nonfiction writer Kaori Hayashii (2005: 32) states that many Japanese women who decided to marry a US soldier had to abandon their plans because parental opposition meant they were unable to obtain an official copy of their family register, which was necessary in order to marry an Occupation soldier. Keiko Tamura, who researched

Japanese women from Kure who married Australian soldiers stationed there during the Occupation, states that she never encountered any women who said their parents and family had agreed to their marriage (2002: 150).

In a situation where, as in the cases discussed in previous chapters, many women were carrying on relationships with Occupation soldiers in secret from their family, or had left home to become involved in the relationship or were in it to make ends meet, it is reassuring to examine cases where women were able to rely completely on their family's support. Even if it turned out that marriage was out of the question, in this situation the economic concerns faced by other women did not exist. Fuji's survival strategy lies in her having persuaded her parents to allow her to marry this soldier.

Fuji's narrative also reveals a discourse strategy. The investigator's note regarding her discussion of her relationship with the Occupation soldier states, 'With tears in her eyes, she commented that "Such a lifestyle is shameful for a Japanese, and it is difficult to face Japanese men"'. Yet the investigator casts some doubt on Fuji's claim. The notes contain a parenthetical comment to the effect that there is a contradiction between Fuji's desire to actively move the relationship toward marriage and her feeling that their liaison is emotionally fraught and shameful. Nevertheless, the investigator's final comment states that Fuji seems like a respectable woman, even though she likes a life of luxury. Even if Fuji gave the investigator the impression that she enjoyed a luxurious lifestyle, she simultaneously conveyed a respectable image, so we can conclude that her discourse strategy was successful.

Women who turned down a marriage proposal

Umeko: taking charge

As an example of a woman who persuaded an Occupation soldier to marry her and to pay for her younger brother's school expenses, let us examine the narrative of Umeko (twenty-one), who worked as a typist at a US base in Tokyo. Umeko became close to this soldier while working at the base. When he was posted to Kyoto, she followed him there. To cover the school expenses of her younger brother, who was attending a high school operating under the new postwar guidelines, Umeko began working as a typist in a life insurance company.

One day, however, an MP pulled Umeko in for a VD check, and although she was let off on that occasion, her company found out about this and sacked her. Umeko's narrative suggests that they dismissed her because they suspected she was a *panpan*, since she had been rounded up for VD testing.

Umeko's boyfriend helped out with her brother's school expenses. At first her brother had been opposed to Umeko's relationship, but he was grateful to the soldier for covering these expenses, which enabled him to attend school. The soldier had expressed his intention to marry Umeko, and he gave her 20,000 yen each month and brought her items such as clothes and candy. His family back home sent her everyday necessities, so their relationship clearly received his family's blessing. Presumably, the fact that Umeko was a Catholic was an important factor behind this approval.

Faced with the overwhelming power imbalance between an Occupation soldier and a member of the occupied nation that prevailed in the contact zone, Umeko adopted the survival strategy of eliciting money and goods from the soldier and his family back home, on the premise of marriage. Although Shunka and Natsume likewise corresponded with their partners' families, it is noteworthy that Umeko also received material assistance from her partner's family.

Discussing her lifestyle with the investigator, Umeko stated that she was thinking solely of her brother and that she had no concerns for herself beyond him graduating and being able to support himself. We can probably view this, however, as an expression of her motives couched in terms acceptable to the investigator. Commenting on the language used to express motivations, Ueno (2018: 29) clearly explains that the range of choices for the 'story' one tells in response to questions about one's motivation is limited. Within these confines, individuals opt for language that describes their motives in a manner that is socially acceptable and to their own advantage. Moreover, the 'motives' offered in such situations are not the actual reasons, but after-the-fact justifications. As a specific example of this, Ueno mentions how when a wife suffering domestic violence says she stays with her husband because she does not want to deprive the children of their father's presence in their lives, society accepts this as self-sacrificial 'maternal love'.

The investigator's notes stated as follows: 'Umeko is a self-professed Catholic and has said God will forgive her for her current lifestyle. I gained the impression that she is highly intelligent, has refined emotions, and is smart. Yet I cannot help but feel that she is in great distress. My impression is of a woman of intellect who is suffering'. Although the investigator has some doubts about Umeko's claims to be a Catholic, Umeko's narrative is acceptable to the investigator, who is in the position of rehabilitating women in a relationship with an Occupation soldier. Even if Umeko's true motives lie elsewhere, the fact that she gave the investigator the impression that she had no option but to enter into a relationship with an Occupation soldier so as to raise money to cover her brother's school expenses – as well as the fact that she emphasized to the investigator that the soldier's family approves of the relationship – meant that the investigator regarded her as having no other options, even if she was a *panpan*. In other words, Umeko convinced the investigator of the validity of her reasons for becoming a *panpan*.

In addition, since Umeko was no longer able to work in an ordinary company because she had been rounded up for a VD check, the financial assistance from the soldier was of great help while her brother attended school. In this respect, we cannot overlook the fact that Umeko targeted a commissioned officer capable of providing sufficient financial support to cover her brother's school expenses. She received 20,000 yen from the soldier each month, and his well-off family back home were able to send things to her. Since Umeko's real reason for associating with an Occupation soldier and dangling the prospect of marriage before him was to receive money and goods, a relationship with an ordinary soldier who sent money back home every month would not have been possible.

Umeko's survival strategy lay in controlling the situation while employing a discourse strategy toward the investigator that differed from the one she adopted with the soldier and his family.

Tsukushi: captivating several soldiers despite no intention of marriage

Tsukushi (eighteen) had a father who was so well off that he could afford three mistresses. When she was four, Tsukushi was adopted by her uncle and aunt. Her biological mother was divorced from Tsukushi's father, leaving behind four children. After Tsukushi graduated from a girls' high school in Kyoto, she entered the Takarazuka Music School, but her father forced her to drop out. She then worked as a typist on a US military base, where she fell in love with a twenty-three-year-old soldier. Tsukushi intended to marry him, but he went home, planning on returning to Japan two months later. Tsukushi then became involved with a different soldier in Maizuru. He too ended up going home, and even though she received a letter saying he would be returning to Japan, Tsukushi started up a relationship with yet another soldier, as had happened in the case of the first soldier. Commenting on Tsukushi's behavior, the investigator observed that 'This course of events suggests that Tsukushi's experience of falling in love with the first soldier served as the trigger for further relationships where her goal was money, so that she gave herself to men and lived with them even though she was not particularly in love with them'. Yet it is inconceivable that Tsukushi, who was good-looking and well educated and worked as a typist on a US base, would move from relationship to relationship in this way purely for financial reasons. The soldiers involved with Tsukushi, who all told her they would return to Japan, wanted to marry her because she came from a high social class.

In this way, after Tsukushi began working as a typist she entered into exclusive relationships with four different soldiers in succession, three of whom were firmly in love with her. The fourth soldier in particular was committed to marrying Tsukushi, and his mother back home also wrote to her, yet Tsukushi herself had no intention of marrying him. When she was in hospital with a VD, the third soldier became involved with a 'whorehouse slut', so Tsukushi broke off their relationship. Even with this soldier, it was Tsukushi who took the initiative in the break-up.

Hajime Kakita (2016: 247) has noted that since before World War II many of the students at Takarazuka Music School were from good families. The fact that Tsukushi's father forced her to drop out from this school shows that his social capital was quite high. In addition to the fact that Tsukushi was beautiful, musically talented and a high school graduate, her school was a Christian one, so she met all the criteria for a woman in occupied Japan to be considered as a potential marriage partner by an Occupation soldier. Tsukushi said that while she was at high school she used to enjoy spending time at cafes. As a result, in the summer vacation she was packed off to spend a month at the home of a relative who was a police chief, where she was pulled into line. This shows that the proper way to behave had been drilled into Tsukushi. These aspects of her background are obvious in the investigator's notes indicating that Tsukushi had a very lively temperament and was chatty and high-spirited and that her upbringing involved old-fashioned strictness. Tsukushi brought these characteristics to her work as a typist at the US base, and it is understandable that it was these very attributes that attracted Occupation soldiers. It is possible that other soldiers also wished to marry Tsukushi.

In this way, the behavior of the soldiers in an intimate relationship with Tsukushi differed from that of the other soldiers discussed so far. Tsukushi was a woman in an occupied nation, while the soldiers she dated were on the victor's side. Yet despite the overwhelming power imbalance between the two parties, Tsukushi had these men wrapped around her little finger.

To Tsukushi, her boyfriends' return home spelled the end of their love, and she soon found her next admirer. She was clearly well aware that as long as the soldier was a member of the victorious military, the center of overwhelming power, a proposal would not necessarily lead to marriage. That is precisely why Tsukushi felt free to toy with the soldiers' feelings and cut ties with them as soon as they returned home. This constitutes the nearest thing to resistance that is available for a woman in a situation of unequal power relations in an occupied nation, and it is one of the few survival options at hand in these circumstances.

Chapter 6

Surviving Experiences on the Continuum of Sexual Violence

Forms of rape, prostitution, love and marriage between Occupation soldiers and women in occupied territories often fall on the continuum of sexual violence. In the course of interviewing battered women, Liz Kelly, who worked at a refuge for these women, found that their experiences of heterosexual acts did not consist of a dichotomy between consent and rape but occurred on a continuum ranging from coercion to force (1987: 48). As a result, she discovered that 'many women experience non-consensual sex which neither they nor the law and, even more unlikely, the man, define as rape' (Kelly 1987: 58).

Commenting on German women who associated with occupying Soviet soldiers after the fall of Berlin in 1945, German historian Atina Grossmann (1995: 54–55) identified 'their own sense of confusion about the fine lines between rape, prostitution, and consensual (albeit generally instrumental) sex'. It is this 'confusion' that clearly reveals that these women are situated on a continuum of sexual violence. Perceiving heterosexual experiences in terms of a binary opposition between consent and rape makes it difficult to understand the specific individual experiences of women in occupied territories who have sexual encounters with members of the occupying forces. Unless the relationship with the soldier is defined as rape, it is interpreted as 'consensual', and even the limited survival strategies by which women can manifest their agency in order to live through this overwhelming power imbalance are boiled down to 'a consensual relationship'.

The case of Kanna (twenty-four), who was working at a cabaret that catered exclusively to Occupation soldiers, lies on the continuum of sexual violence between rape and sex work. In November 1945, when Kanna was twenty and working at K Cabaret, she was taken by a friend to a bedroom at the cabaret. Her friend regularly serviced Occupation soldiers as clients, but Kanna was a virgin, and it was the first time she had taken an Occupation soldier as a client. The soldier Kanna was with thought she worked in 'the business', and he raped her before tossing her fifty yen and leaving. Kanna told the investigator that even now she is bitter about how her virginity was stolen. Given the fact that the starting salary of a bank clerk in 1945 was eighty yen per month (*Shukan Asahi*, ed., 1995: 61), fifty yen was by no means a trifling sum at the time, but the amount of money is not the issue here. Kanna did not view herself as being 'in the business', but when the soldier threw the money at her she *became* part of 'the business'. In other words, there is a cognitive dissonance between the soldier's view of this act as prostitution, not rape, and Kanna's perception that it was rape, not prostitution. It is this very difference in perception that reveals the continuum of sexual violence between rape and sex work. Nevertheless, as Kelly (1987: 48) stresses, it is important to note that it is not a continuum in straight line, but a compound assemblage of various events and experiences.

Considering the power imbalance between Occupation soldiers and Japanese women in terms of the concept of a contact zone allows us to identify the women's strategies for surviving experiences on the continuum of sexual violence. In the first part of this chapter, we see how women survived experiences on the continuum of sexual violence perpetrated by one soldier, while the second part examines their experiences when several soldiers were involved.

Surviving a continuum of sexual violence involving one soldier

Anne: in an exclusive relationship with her rapist

After Anne was tricked and then raped by an Occupation soldier she had met at the cabaret where she worked (see Chapter 2), she came to Kyoto and provided sexual services to only this soldier. He worked as a gate guard at O American military facility in Kyoto (thought to be the Okazaki base). She continued to be involved exclusively with her rapist, receiving money from him when she was experiencing financial difficulties. Because she continued interacting with him, the soldier who raped Anne became her source of income.

According to Anne, he told her would take her to a hotel on the way home from the cabaret, which turned out to be a *ryokan* (Japanese inn) where he robbed her of her virginity. This can be interpreted in light of the number of women raped by an Occupation soldier with overwhelming power over them who were compelled to accept the situation without taking any money.

If, however, we understand Anne's relationship with her rapist in terms of the concept of the contact zone, we see that not only did Anne *not* meekly put up with the situation, but she adopted the survival strategy of demanding money from the soldier who had raped her. Moreover, she negotiated with him to provide him exclusively with sexual services and continued eliciting money from him. If we also apply the lens of a continuum of sexual violence to her ongoing relationship with her rapist, whose exclusive prostitute she became, it is impossible to conclude that the rape / sex work / love relationship between them was 'consensual'. We cannot ignore the fact that Anne was raped by the soldier with whom she was subsequently in a relationship.

Anne claimed to the investigator that she was not a *panpan*, saying she would like a distinction to be drawn between an 'only one' like herself, who did not have a VD, and women from whorehouses (brothels) and that she would like to be given a card stating she was free of venereal disease. This argument was a survival strategy used by Anne so that her behavior and actions would not be stigmatized by society's perception that she became a *panpan* after being raped.

Tamako: diverse discourse strategies

Let us turn now to Tamako (nineteen), who told the investigator that even if she continued her relationship with an Occupation soldier, she could not marry him. Tamako was from Nagano prefecture, where she had dropped out of girls' high school. A volleyball friend from her school days was working as a cabaret dancer in Yokohama, so Tamako also became a dancer there. She met T at the cabaret and became involved with him, but he was posted to Osaka. When Tamako was ill in bed, this soldier sent her clothes, accessories and 4,000 yen. The fact that he also sent dozens of letters shows he was very much in love with her. After Tamako rejected T's marriage proposal, in his grief he caused a public disturbance in a drunken stupor and was thrown into the lockup for two months. Tamako said their relationship continued after he was released, with T visiting her lodgings twice a week.

Tamako told the investigator that 'It would be difficult to marry T, and I'm worried about what the future holds. I'd like to learn a handicraft so that I can support myself' – yet she continued her relationship with T. After he was released from the lockup, Tamako resigned from the Yokohama cabaret where she had been making quite a good living and moved to Kyoto. In Kyoto, she said, 'My daily needs are met, but I'm bored when T doesn't come to see me, so I help the woman who runs the place where I'm staying and go shopping with her or play with the little kids at my lodgings'. Tamako's father had died the year the war ended, and her older brother had died in the war. Her remaining family consisted of her three older sisters (one of whom was married), her younger brother and her mother. There is no indication that Tamako sent money to her family. She also commented that 'If I were to go out by myself, people would probably call me a *panpan*, so I make sure that when I do go out, it's always with my landlady'. She was clearly taking care not to be regarded as a *panpan*. Meanwhile, Tamako's description of her lifestyle, wherein T visited her twice a week, as 'letting matters drag on' indicates that she continued the relationship with him for financial reasons.

The investigator seemed to like Tamako. Their notes describe her as having a 'gentle temperament. She is not a brazen hussy. She has a strong desire to start out afresh. Healthy'. This view is the complete opposite of the investigator's appraisal of Lily (twenty-three), a sex worker at a brothel, who says, 'I won't stop working as a *panpan* unless I'm rounded up'. The investigator describes her as having 'dreadful looks, so with that face and appearance it's amazing that anyone goes to see her. She is a typical streetwalker to her very core'.

The investigator's attitude toward Tamako reveals that Tamako was working to shape the narrative to make the investigator view her in a positive light. In short, when describing her motivation Tamako uses language that is palatable to the investigator. It is likely that she also employs a discourse strategy that is acceptable to T. This would account for why, even though Tamako refused to marry him, T continued to support her with enough money and gifts to live on. This is what differentiates Tamako from Lily, who did not employ any discourse strategies. Lily spoke boldly to the investigator of the 'fun' she was having. She said, 'Of course I love alcohol and cigarettes, but I really enjoy being a woman of the night, and there's no way I could give it up', indicating that rather than sleeping exclusively with just one soldier she preferred to make money off many soldiers. As a result, the investigator described Lily as a 'typical streetwalker'.[1] By contrast, Tamako managed to avoid the 'typical street-walker' label even while still carrying on her relationship with a soldier.

Because Tamako's narrative of her relationship with T moves back and forth along the continuum of sex work, love and marriage, it is difficult to identify her survival strategy. Yet her very behavior in actively deploying a range of discourse strategies can be regarded as her survival strategy.

Surviving a continuum of sexual violence involving several soldiers

Sakurako: raped, disowned, then engaged

Different Occupation soldiers were involved in the continuum of sexual violence surrounding Sakurako (twenty-one). After completing elementary school, Sakurako attended a nurses' training school. While working as a nurse, she was raped by two Occupation soldiers on her way home from work one day (as described in Chapter 2).

Sakurako was raped in March 1946, just before she turned nineteen. After completing elementary school, she had enrolled in nurses' training school and became a nurse at K.K. Center. During her assault, even though Sakurako screamed and fought back, nobody noticed what was happening. Her 'moralistic' father, instead of standing up for her, forced her to resign from her job. As a result, Sakurako had an argument with him five months after she was raped by the soldiers, and she left home.

Sakurako repeatedly used her own body, which had been sexually assaulted by the victors, to earn money, saying 'I searched for tricks everywhere and made some money. I went back home in December, but I didn't stop servicing johns'.

After leaving home, Sakurako began to attend a Catholic church in Kawaramachi Sanjo in Kyoto every Sunday. She said, 'I'm currently in love with a soldier, and although he's back home now, he's applying for permission to marry me'. It is not known when and where she met this man. He introduced Sakurako to a waitressing job that paid 4,000 yen per month, a good wage considering the starting salary of an elementary school teacher at the time was 2,000 yen per month.

Let us consider this situation from a contact zone perspective. In the first place, Sakurako is undeniably a victim of violence and rape by Occupation soldiers, in an overwhelmingly asymmetrical power relationship. Further, she was disowned by her father because of the rape, and was no longer able to live at home. Yet Sakurako was not a powerless victim. She subsequently earned money through repeated encounters with many different Occupation soldiers, and eventually she not only found work as a waitress through one particular soldier, but even elicited a promise of marriage from him. Her excellent negotiating skills constitute Sakurako's survival strategy.

Tsubaki: on the offensive after a forced miscarriage

Tsubaki (aged nineteen) was in a relationship with an Occupation soldier. When she had a miscarriage, he accused her of deliberately causing it, so she left him. When Tsubaki became pregnant to a second Occupation soldier, she took some white pills he gave her and had another miscarriage. Such experiences were no doubt not unusual due to the overwhelming power imbalance between occupier and occupied. If, however, we view the encounter between Tsubaki and these soldiers as a contact zone, we see that Tsubaki did not remain passive after these bitter experiences. Instead, she embarked on a counterattack.

After being forced to take some white pills and having a miscarriage, Tsubaki broke things off with the second soldier and returned home, taking up work as a freelance hostess in Kyoto. She says that during this time she was rounded up on several occasions, and 'in desperation' she was unfaithful. This 'infidelity' involved affairs with four Occupation soldiers. Because these affairs were going on simultaneously, Tsubaki would have the soldiers visit her lodgings at set times, so that they would not bump into each other. If the soldiers did run into each other at the entrance to her place, they would get into fierce arguments over Tsubaki, so she would hole up inside. Since Tsubaki describes these four affairs as a matter of 'infidelity', the line between sex work and love in this case is blurry.

After her involvement with these four men, Tsubaki entered into a relationship with an Occupation soldier who was in Otsu and had him give her 30,000 yen each month. That was quite a sum for an exclusive sexual relationship with just one man. Tsubaki did not mention how she felt toward this soldier. In other words, it is again unclear whether her relationship with him was transactional or a love relationship.

As stated earlier, Tamako's relationship with T moved back and forth along the continuum of sexual violence between sex work, love and marriage. Similarly, Tsubaki also shifted between prostitution and love. The difference between the two women is that Tamako was vacillating in her relationship with a single soldier (T), whereas Tsubaki did so along the continuum of sex work and love with several soldiers. In the process, she steadily bolstered her survival strategy. Even if Tsubaki was found to be simultaneously involved with four different men, none of them subjected her to violence, and she ultimately acquired a different soldier as an even better source of income. This was how Tsubaki, who had been forced to take white pills to abort a pregnancy, launched her counteroffensive.

Hamana: manipulating different soldiers

Hamana (seventeen), with whom we conclude this chapter, was the youngest of the sixty-three women studied here. Amidst the overwhelming power imbalance between Occupation soldiers and women in occupied Japan, it was Hamana who best symbolized the contact zone and made the most of her negotiating abilities to maximize her survival strategy.

The timeline of Hamana's involvement with Occupation soldiers started when she met a soldier at the end of 1945. He proposed to her in front of her adoptive mother, and soon after that she worked as a *panpan* in a brothel for Occupation soldiers for a year. Sometime around March 1948, she became exclusive to a particular soldier. As detailed below, Hamana also represents an unusual case that cannot be explained in similar terms to those of the other women discussed so far.

Pushy proposal, but relationship peters out

When Hamana was four years old, she had been adopted by a friend of her father. This friend lived in the historic

Higashiyama district in Kyoto, and Hamana's life there was a comfortable one in a house surrounded by a traditional wall. Her father worked as a government official in another town, and he too was well off. Because of her strict adoptive mother, Hamana dropped out of girls' high school. Her interactions with the soldier who proposed to her started when Hamana was walking across Shijo Ohashi Bridge in Kyoto one day and a *panpan* came up and asked if she was a *panpan*.

When Hamana said no, the woman introduced her to an Occupation soldier. He took her to a room for rent, where they had sex. It is unclear how long Hamana was involved with this soldier after that, but she started work at a brothel the following month, so it would likely have been just a matter of days. After Hamana told this soldier where her 'real house' was, he made his way there after asking for assistance from a local police officer in Shirakawa. This indicates that when Hamana was involved with Occupation soldiers at that time, she would provide them with a false address. She probably also gave a false name.

The soldier who went to Hamana's home with the local policeman proposed to her. In front of her adoptive mother, he asked Hamana to marry him, saying he would obtain permission from his mother, who was in Okayama prefecture.

Occupation forces were first stationed in Okayama when a US advance party arrived on 12 October 1945, and by the following month about 5,000 personnel were stationed there (Sunamoto et al., 2016: 713). In February 1946, the Department of the Army gave permission for dependents of Occupation personnel to enter Japan (Ando and Sasamoto 1996: 33), so the soldier's mother was clearly already in Japan before such permission was granted. Because rank-and-file soldiers lived in camps, there was no way they could have their mothers visit from back home. The fact that the soldier who proposed to Hamana visited her home with the help of a policeman also suggests that he was a commissioned officer. His visit to the home of Hamana's adoptive parents to ask for her hand in marriage suggests that after finding out information about Hamana without her knowledge he had concluded that she was suited to become his wife.

Hamana's adoptive mother was shocked to learn that Hamana had taken up with an Occupation soldier. After he left, Hamana's adoptive mother angrily said, 'I wondered why you were always coming home late, and now it turns out that you were messing about with [REDACTED]. You've brought shame on the family name'. She tearfully added, 'You've turned out to be a good-for-nothing daughter. If you want to stay in this house, stop seeing [REDACTED]'. Even considering that the soldier who proposed to Hamana was of a sufficiently high rank that the policeman showed him how to find her house, to Hamana's adoptive mother he was still from a former enemy nation. Her reaction was the complete opposite to that in the case of Fuji (Chapter 5), who persuaded both her parents to agree to her marriage to an Occupation soldier. Fuji was also from a well-off family, but unlike Fuji's parents, Hamana's adoptive mother refused to give permission for Hamana to marry an Occupation soldier.

When her adoptive mother opposed the marriage, Hamana initially replied 'I'm going to marry [REDACTED]', but her relationship with this soldier was already tapering off, so she actually had no intention of doing so. Because her adoptive mother was overly strict, Hamana said she no longer wanted to remain in that house.

Hamana's behavior in dating an Occupation soldier despite having no desire to marry him calls to mind American 'charity girls' around the turn of the twentieth century. According to Chiori Goto, who is an expert on the subject, American charity girls were characteristically aged from their mid-teens into their mid-twenties and employed as department store workers, factory laborers, domestic help, waitresses, stenographers, telephone operators and so on. Goto (2017: 50–51) writes that in their spare time they wore bold clothing and makeup and, acting alone or in pairs away from their parents' eyes, they gathered at commercial recreational facilities such as dance halls, theaters, restaurants, bars, ice-cream parlors, parks, amusement parks and pleasure boats. There the charity girls would engage intimately with men. According to Goto, these young women held certain tenets, and in return for a 'fun time' with men at an amusement facility, they not only engaged in sexual acts in the strict sense but sometimes simply flaunted their sex appeal. Above all, charity girls emphasized the principle of not accepting money (Goto 2017: 52). In other words, they did not seek financial compensation for sex work. Goto concludes that what charity girls sought when flaunting their sex appeal was not money but a 'fun time' here and there, and they had not necessarily fallen into 'sexual immorality' as a result of outright poverty (2017: 56). This also applies to Hamana, who was from a well-off family and dropped out of girls' high school because of her adoptive mother's strictness. When Hamana was mobilized as a student to work at a factory during the war, her adoptive mother found out that she had chatted on the train with a student from a secondary school for men under the old educational system, who had likewise been mobilized. Hamana relates how she was scolded and beaten, which prompted her to drop out of high school and leave home. To Hamana, her relationship with the Occupation soldier allowed her to forget about her strict adoptive mother, and the fact that she was not seeking financial compensation in her relationship is reminiscent of the situation with charity girls.

In other words, it was because Hamana had no intention of marrying the Occupation soldier and because her involvement with him was merely a means to get away from her strict adoptive mother that she put an end to the relationship. Hamana's survival strategy entailed using her involvement with an Occupation soldier as a means to escape her adoptive mother.

Gifts from client soldiers

After winding down her relationship with this soldier, Hamana then took on clients at a brothel.

> Seven or eight *panpan* worked there. It was a two-story house, and in those days a one-time stand cost from 300 to 400 yen, while an all-nighter cost as much as 2,000 yen. If a client became attached to me, he would give me shoes, stockings, underwear and other gifts, and I also received candy and food. Servicing johns meant having up to four clients in the space of twenty-four hours. So far, I've had sex with about 500 men. Probably because I'm young, I don't get tired. I'm tiny, so the johns call me Shorty. Because I'm so small, they took pity on me, and some even left money without having sex with me. I looked so young that when they asked how old I am and I replied sixteen [by the traditional Japanese count], they would say I must really be eight or nine.

Here Hamana provides an important hint for understanding the soldiers she serviced in this private house turned brothel. In addition to the set fee, the soldiers would give 'other gifts' to their regulars. Because the brothel was in Shijo Kawaramachi and the soldiers who were clients there gave her 'other gifts' in addition to the sex-work fee, it most likely was a brothel where commissioned officers gathered. Handing over 'other gifts' on top of the set fee to women they were close to was possible only for commissioned officers with some financial discretion. They could easily afford to give the women not only 'candy and food' but also shoes, stockings and underwear. Moreover, given Hamana's statement that 'I'm so small, they took pity on me, and some even left money without having sex with me', it seems that many of the soldiers who came to the brothel where Hamana worked were 'principled' and high-minded.

A statement made by Waka (age unknown) contrasts with Hamana's comments above. When Waka was in the second year of girls' high school, she failed to progress to the next year because of missing too much school due to illness, so she transferred to a girls' vocational school. Around the time of her graduation, she was raped by a friend of her older brother. Waka's father worked at K electrical company and was a contractor, and Waka had been attending a girls' high school, so her family was relatively well off. When Waka was working at a beer hall, she was rounded up for a VD check and sent to a hospital, where she met a woman who ended up stealing her watch and shoes. To earn money to buy new ones, Waka left home and worked at a brothel and had relations with Occupation soldiers for about two months. The upshot was that 'In the two months I was there, far from earning money I racked up 9,000 yen in debts, so I got fed up with it'.

By contrast, Hamana gives the impression that she enjoyed working at the brothel. She was fourteen or fifteen years old by Western reckoning while working there, and some Occupation soldiers who bought her services might have had a daughter back home the same age as her, who looked like she was ten or even younger. While it would be mistaken to conclude that all commissioned officers who had a wife and children took on a lover in occupied Japan, some certainly did. Some probably used a brothel precisely because they did have a wife and children.

We should not overlook the fact that Hamana spoke of working at the brothel in positive terms, which can be largely attributed to the fact that her family was well off. That is why Hamana's narrative contains no mention of financial stress, which is precisely why she apparently enjoyed the brothel work. Moreover, since Hamana went to the brothel on the introduction of a 'friend who is a *panpan*', it is likely that her friend was also from a similar background. We can conclude, therefore, that the brothel where Hamana worked was one where commissioned officers would gather and leave lavish tips, and this was another reason why Hamana found it rewarding to work there.

Love triangle

Let us focus now on the time when Hamana was in an exclusive relationship with an Occupation soldier. The trigger for this was the fact that around March 1948 there was a drastic increase in roundups by MPs. Facing difficulties after having often been rounded up, Hamana went to Nishi-Maizuru on the recommendation of a housemate. She worked at a bar there for four or five days, and then left her lodgings there without permission and met M, an Occupation soldier, at a dance hall in Higashi-Maizuru. She moved in with M in April.

Now that Hamana had become exclusive with M in Higashi-Maizuru and was receiving 40,000 yen from him each month, her lifestyle was supported. She set off for Kyoto several days before M was due to go there on fifteen-days of leave. Presumably she intended to spend time with M during his free time. Hamana arrived in Kyoto a week before M, and while enjoying herself at a dance hall she became close to another soldier who worked with M, and began a relationship with him. The important point here is that Hamana was not invited into an exclusive relationship with M's buddy as a dancer, but while enjoying herself as a customer. Perhaps it was due to the fact that Hamana had enough money to have a good time at the Higashi-Maizuru dance hall where she met M that she was able to have a relationship with him.

Someone able to hand over 40,000 yen a month is clearly not a rank-and-file soldier. The fact that Hamana's adoptive mother was very strict also indicates that Hamana must have been taught to behave properly from when she was a young child. After encountering various women in occupied Japan, M perhaps sensed from Hamana's behavior that she came from a privileged background. Perhaps too he realized that Hamana, who also had the money she earned in the brothel, was not driven solely by financial motives. Arguably, this was exactly why M desired a relationship with her. Even the fact that M's buddy became involved with Hamana despite knowing of her relationship with M was perhaps because he was attracted by Hamana's economic freedom and motivated by a desire to steal her away from M if he had a chance. Ultimately, M was two-timed by Hamana.

It is noteworthy that, despite the overwhelming power imbalance between Occupation soldiers and the women of occupied Japan, seventeen-year-old Hamana had successive Occupation soldiers and commissioned officers wrapped around her little finger.

Chapter 7

Marriage to an
Occupation Soldier

Occupation soldiers were an object of fascination not only for women in defeated Japan but also for men and children. Thus, this chapter discusses marriage with Occupation soldiers in light of their relationships with women in occupied Japan and compares the situation in Japan with that in occupied France.

The allure of Occupation soldiers

In the eyes of Kazuya Kosaka: laughing blonde lads

Kazuya Kosaka, a rockabilly singer who took Japan by storm in the 1950s and was later also a successful actor, wrote a memoir of the Occupation in Japanese, titled *Meido in okyupaido Jyapan* (Made in occupied Japan; 1990). In this book Kosaka, who was born in 1935, described the US soldiers he saw when in fourth grade – just after the end of World War II – as follows:

> I saw a crowd of people, more than fifty. Despite the number, they were all well-behaved, cheerfully gazing up at the top of a stone wall.
>
> Wondering what was going on, I wandered over to take a look. Even now, over four decades later, I vividly remember that scene.
>
> About a dozen US soldiers were perched in a row on the stone wall as if sunbathing, and they were gazing down at us. Wearing khaki jackets (possibly battle uniforms) with several large pockets, and some wearing a khaki-colored cap while others were bareheaded, they were dangling their legs clad in sturdy-looking military boots and chatting away with each other while occasionally glancing down at the

crowd of Japanese below, making comments and laughing out loud.

To me, just an elementary school kid, it felt like standing in front of a wild animal's cage at the zoo for the first time, but I plucked up the courage to mingle with the crowd.

The US soldiers did not seem as grown-up as I'd expected, so it is quite appropriate to call them "lads". Their blonde hair shone against the backdrop of the blue sky. They had blue eyes that were constantly moving and white (actually pink) faces, and their noses seemed especially prominent, perhaps because I was looking up at them from below. Of course, I didn't have a clue as to what they were saying to each other, but they spoke in loud, cheerful voices, and above all they laughed a lot. (Kosaka 1990: 10)

The soldiers were so young that Kosaka, who was still in elementary school, thought they were less grown-up than he had expected them to be. Kosaka had been evacuated to Nagoya, his father's hometown, with his mother and younger sister and brother. His father had stayed in Tokyo because of his job.

The Japanese congregating around the stone wall were there in the hope of getting their hands on some of the black-market goods the US soldiers had brought from their base (mostly chocolate, chewing gum, cigarettes and so on). Kosaka remembered the scene as follows:

In response to requests from the crowd, the US soldiers on the wall would produce stuff from their pockets like a magician and enter into cheerful haggling over the price. There was no sign of the antipathy expected between Americans and Japanese – the victors and the defeated, who until just recently had been enemies. Watching the carryings-on of the Americans, who engaged with us in a very easy manner or even on equal terms, made me too break out in a smile. (1990: 11)

With both sides – the victorious soldiers on top of the wall and the defeated Japanese below – laughing away as they haggled with each other, the 'wall' separating them served as a veritable contact zone enabling negotiations between occupiers and occupied.

After witnessing this scene, Kosaka went to see the soldiers on the wall every day. He was fascinated by the negotiations, but he also had misgivings. When he plucked up the courage to tell his mother about what was happening, he found out that she had long known about the situation. Thinking he had nothing to lose, Kosaka asked his mother if they too could buy something, and she gave him money to get chocolate for himself and his siblings. He headed straight off to the wall, where he started bargaining with the soldiers over the price of chocolate.

"Haroo".

"Have you chocolate?"

"How much!"

It was all very easy, even something of an anticlimax. Three Milky Way chocolates that looked just like gold bars dropped heavily into my outstretched hands. The US soldiers treated me exactly like the grown-up men who were regulars there, even though I was still in fourth grade and this was the first time I'd ever tried to speak English. (Kosaka 1990: 14)

In Japan, where there was an overwhelming power imbalance between occupiers and occupied, Kosaka negotiated with the young Occupation soldiers on an equal footing, just like their adult regulars. To the young Kosaka, the US soldiers seemed like 'blonde lads who laughed a lot'.[1]

No doubt the 'allure' of the 'laughing blonde lads' was not limited to Kosaka and the 'grown-up regulars' but was also felt by some women in occupied Japan.

Kosaka's mother was already aware of the details of the interactions on the wall: she knew 'not only was I going to the wall every day to check out what was going on but also of what the US soldiers were selling there, the prices and nearly everything it took me days to figure out' (1990: 12). She knew all this because she'd heard about it from the women in her neighborhood (1990: 12). The food situation during the Occupation was grim: 'In cities, it was difficult to get hold even of potatoes unless you went to the countryside to buy them, and even if you were finally able to get your hands on some, on the way home you might be unlucky enough to get caught up in a sweeping police crackdown and have everything confiscated' (1990: 17). In those circumstances, the goods the US soldiers brought along, such as soap and food, appealed not only to Kosaka and the adult men who were regulars at the wall, but also to women, such as Kosaka's mother and her neighbors. The relationship between Kosaka, his mother and the Occupation soldiers raises some interesting points.

Masakazu Tanaka is a cultural anthropologist who regards Japanese society during the Occupation as a contact zone and who has carried out research on '*panpan*', with a focus on Japanese intellectuals, activists and children. He has pointed out the need to take 'intermediaries' in contact zones into consideration, suggesting that perhaps we should adopt the view that countless intermediaries and mediators are at work between the dominant and dominated (Tanaka 2011b: 164, 182).[2] Kosaka, who negotiated directly with the US soldiers, clearly fulfilled the role of an 'intermediary' between the soldiers and Kosaka's mother, who did not negotiate with them in person. It is possible that the men who were regulars might also have been procuring goods from the US soldiers as 'intermediaries' acting on behalf of their wives and mothers.

If we look at things in this light, we can conclude that, through such 'intermediaries', women in occupied Japan who had no direct contact with the occupiers were involved in negotiations with the 'laughing blonde lads' of the Occupation. To these women, these 'lads' were 'fascinating' young men who were the bearers of a foreign culture. At the same time, they were also occupiers who symbolized wealth and power – as well as violence.

In the eyes of a policeman-interpreter: stylish MPs

In my book *Who Were Panpan?* (Chazono 2014: 81), I described the diverse ways in which Japanese men who had experienced defeat in World War II viewed Occupation soldiers, as well as the differences in what they saw. The MP interpreter Hiroshi Harada who was mentioned in the introduction to this book touches on aspects not found in the narratives of education critic Kiyoshi Kanzaki and researchers at the Kyoto Social Welfare Research Center, which published *Streetwalkers*, a book that presents the findings of the survey I examined in my book. Whereas Kanzaki and the center researchers turned a critical eye on Occupation soldiers (Chazono 2014), Harada admired their stylishness and how, unlike Japanese military officers, the officers treated the soldiers under them with respect.

Harada, who had worked alongside Occupation soldiers, wrote as follows:

To a man, the MPs were smartly dressed. They were tall, and they looked good in their uniforms. In particular, their shoes were so shiny. I had them teach me how to polish shoes. After applying shoe cream, you spray on water – if you don't have any water on hand, use spit – and then rub it in with a cloth. This gave the shoes a lustrous black shine. Since we policemen had never seen anyone spit on their shoes before, we looked at each other in surprise, saying "Wow, that's pretty incredible". (2011: 49)

The soldiers' 'stylishness' remained vivid in Harada's mind even sixty years after the end of the war.

Harada also recalled how the victorious soldiers had the mental capacity to respond to heckling from the defeated Japanese in a laid-back manner.

Protesters occasionally yelled out "Yankee go home!" I heard a waggish MP laughingly reply, "Oh, yes. You're right. I want to go home too". And that made *me* laugh. Because the atmosphere was so light-hearted, there was no sense of tension when a gum-chewing MP radioed into military police headquarters, and things even seemed peaceful. (Harada 2011: 49–52)

It is easy to picture the soldier responding with humor to the 'Yankee' insult. This was only possible because of the luxury of being in the victor's position.

They [the soldiers] all took pride in their work and showed no shame about it. If someone were to ask a Japanese what his job is, would he proudly reply that he is a farmer or factory worker, a driver or woodcutter? Despite claiming there is no superior or inferior when it comes to jobs,

Japanese would in reality surely hesitate for a moment. Most of the MPs responded proudly when asked what their old job was back home, happily saying they would return to it once their military service was over. (Harada 1994: 95)

Harada's comment indicates that the MPs, who were in a position of power in occupied Japan, included some who were not from a privileged class back home. This reminds us of the soldier who promised to marry Yuri, who was from a good family, who said he 'drove cars for a living' back home (see Chapter 5).

Harada also noted that relations between the soldiers and their superiors were closer than in the Japanese army and that he often saw commissioned officers and rank-and-file soldiers outside of work hours chatting familiarly or taking a walk together. 'This was a huge difference from the situation in the Imperial Japanese Army, where it was common for non-commissioned officers to hit or kick rank-and-file soldiers' (Harada 1994: 126).

A student in the fifth grade of elementary school described similar treatment in an essay about his father's life in the Japanese army.

If a soldier didn't polish his shoes properly or didn't salute a superior or he screwed up in some way, he'd be hit in the face until he went bright red, and on top of that he'd be made to run around the perimeter of the barracks. [...] When fainthearted soldiers were made to do such things over and over, they apparently died by their own hand.

My dad told me that once he got such bad heatstroke he nearly died, and at that time his squad leader repeatedly hit him on the side of his face. It must have really hurt.

Such stories make me realize that the Japanese army must have done very bad things. At the same time, I remembered American soldiers. When I was walking around the Isezakicho shopping district [in Yokohama], lots of US soldiers would pass by, but I rarely saw any soldiers saluting. […] I wondered why former Japanese soldiers had done such cruel things. I also sometimes wonder why American soldiers are so free by comparison.[3] (Shimizu, Miyahara and Ueda 1953: 100–101)

One day when this student was playing with a friend on the street, they said 'Haroo' to a passing American soldier, and he gave them some chewing gum, so the student thought 'He's nice. I wish he'd always come by here'. The student probably told his family about this when he got home, and that likely prompted his father to talk about his own days in the military.

Harada remarked that 'There's no way you can win a war by being stingy or treating people poorly. I felt strongly that Japan lost to America more because of how its people interact than because of its inferior resources and inferior scientific strength' (1994: 126). After working with the 'stylish' MPs from the victorious Occupation forces, Harada was no doubt able to observe Japan's own military from an objective perspective. The same goes for the father who criticized the army in which he himself had served. Surely it was precisely because he had witnessed the everyday behavior of soldiers from the winning nation that he was able to relativize the actions of Japan's own military.

(Not) speaking of romance

Marriage means freedom to mention the relationship

Etsuko Takushi Crissey, a former reporter with the *Okinawa Times*, interviewed women who moved to the US after marrying a soldier or a civilian in military employ who had been stationed in Okinawa. Takushi Crissey (2017: 52–53) observes that 'I often asked women what had attracted them about their husbands […]. American soldiers seemed so gentle, courteous, caring, and honest toward women. Many other women I interviewed gave the same answer'. Some of the reasons for the attraction were given as follows:

> American soldiers opened doors for women getting into cars or going outside, they carried heavy packages for them, and they pulled out chairs for them to sit down. From the time of their first meeting with American soldiers, women were amazed and deeply impressed by such good manners.
>
> "Whenever I was lost in thought, he'd ask if something was worrying me," one told me.
>
> "It made me happy that he always showed his love for me," said another.
>
> Shōko (California, age mid-sixties) met her husband when she was working as a bus conductor in Okinawa. At first, she was surprised by his aroma: When I approached him to sell the ticket, he smelled like soap. In those days few homes had baths, so people went to the public bath a few times a week. Soap just wasn't available. On rainy days when the bus windows were closed, the passengers' body odor filled the air inside and made it hard to breathe.

The final case above is that of a woman who met her US soldier husband while working as a bus conductor immediately after the war. The bus could be described as their contact zone. They had the opportunity to pursue a romance because the woman had the social capital associated with being a bus company employee.

Tamura (2002: 152) describes the impressions of two Japanese women when they first met and were attracted to Australian soldiers whom they later married, eventually moving to Australia with them.

> A woman who became acquainted with an Australian soldier who visited the newspaper branch where she worked in Tokushima went out with him. They then lived together, having two children before eventually marrying. She said that when she first met the soldier his broken Japanese seemed really cute, so she felt drawn to him.
>
> Another woman whose friend introduced her to the Australian soldier in Kure who later became her husband said she was attracted by how he was an all-round athlete and by his blonde hair and crystal-clear light blue eyes.

The first woman met her future husband at a newspaper company in Tokushima prefecture, while the second met hers through a friend's introduction. The first woman possessed the social capital associated with working in a newspaper company, while the second's social network in the form of a friend introduced her to the foreign soldier. Tamura (2002: 152) concludes that 'The Occupation soldiers were tall and extremely upbeat, and they wore their uniforms stylishly and seemed nice to women. If such a man was interested in dating them, young women would naturally feel some attraction'. Occupation soldiers' good manners and good looks are also mentioned in a composition by a first-year middle school (junior high) student from Maizuru, Kyoto. 'Mom, all sailors are slim gentlemen, aren't they?' (Shimizu, Miyahara and Ueda 1953: 306). This girl wrote about how on the way home from town with her mother one day she saw five or six foreign sailors having fun on a seesaw in a playground she often visited. The foreigners seemed like 'slim gentlemen' to her, so they too were soldiers who 'wore their uniforms stylishly'.

These impressions of the initial encounter with Occupation soldiers as portrayed by women who later married them and presented in the findings of Takushi Crissey and Tamura share similarities with the 'extremely upbeat' part of the description by MP interpreter Harada when discussing Occupation soldiers in relation to the public protest. His impression of the soldiers – 'tall, and they looked good in their uniforms' – also agrees with Tamura's findings on the views of women who married them. Takushi Crissey (2017: 53) acknowledges that 'To be sure, their kind ways, sweet words, and generous gifts were calculated to lure women, but with the grim conditions in Okinawa at the time, women were undeniably impressed'.

There was an overwhelming power imbalance between superiors and inferiors in both the Occupation forces and the Japanese military. In the Japanese case, however, it seems that the act of someone in power treating a powerless person with respect was regarded as 'shameful'. That is why 'it was common for non-commissioned officers to hit or kick rank-and-file soldiers', as Harada (1994: 126) observed. This attitude was further reinforced by the gender norms in Japan. The Occupation, however, witnessed the arrival of men who had defeated Japanese men in war and who treated Japanese women with respect, even though these women were on the losing side. Moreover, Occupation men had overwhelming 'wealth and power'. Nevertheless, we should not forget that, as is evident in this book, the occupiers were armed and sometimes perpetrated sexual violence, depending on the circumstances.

One shared attribute of the Japanese women who became intimately involved with an Occupation soldier and later related the story of their romance to Takushi Crissey or Tamura is that they all legally married the soldier. They could speak freely of how in occupied Japan they met the soldier who became their husband and had a romantic relationship with him that led to marriage.

What, then, of cases where the relationship did *not* lead to marriage?

Non-marriage restricts freedom to mention the romance

Throughout this book I have described how an overwhelming majority of the sixty-three women who were part of the *Streetwalkers* survey told an investigator about their romance with an Occupation soldier.

As noted in the previous section, Takushi Crissey found that the shared reason among US soldier brides for being attracted to US soldiers was that they were 'gentle, courteous, caring, and honest'. These shared attributes are also apparent in the narratives of the women classified as 'streetwalkers' by the Kyoto Social Welfare Research Center.

Let us examine the narratives of three of the women who participated in the *Streetwalkers* survey who spoke about the Occupation soldiers with whom they were involved.

> When Tamako (nineteen) was in bed with abdominal pain and swelling, her boyfriend who had been posted from Yokohama to Osaka sent her clothes and other items, as well as 4,000 yen and dozens of letters.

While Nanoka (twenty-one) was in hospital with a venereal disease, her boyfriend brought her chocolates, cigarettes, bread and butter, as well as meals. "I was so happy, and I don't forget nothin' about that time. He came to visit me every single day".

When Marika (twenty-one) was likewise hospitalized with a venereal disease, she frequently received gifts from her boyfriend in the form of sweets and fruit and so on, as well as love letters, all delivered by her landlady.

What these women had in common was the fact that when they were weak from illness the soldiers they were dating reacted quickly and thoughtfully. When the soldiers were not able to visit their girlfriends, they sent gifts and letters, and when they could visit the hospital, they did so every day and took them meals. When someone is not feeling well, such kindness is bound to touch the heart. There is little difference between how the women who married Occupation soldiers and those whose relationships did not result in marriage look back on their romance.

There is, however, one vast difference between these two groups of women – namely, their ability to talk freely of their romance. Whereas the women who married could mention the romance with their husband freely at any time, those women who did not marry their soldier-boyfriend became less and less able to talk openly of the romance after they had separated, even if they had been able to do so while they were in love. The reason behind this is that when their intimate relationships with Occupation soldiers did not lead to marriage, they suffered the social stigma of being regarded as 'panpan'.

In my book *Who Were Panpan?* I mentioned 'Love letter alley' (Koibumi Yokocho) (Chazono 2014: 19–20), based on Satoko Akio's book *Washinton Haitsu: GHQ ga Tokyo ni kizanda sengo* (Washington Heights: GHQ, engraved in Tokyo after World War II; 2011). Here I would like to revisit this topic based on a *Yomiuri shimbun* article dated 23 November 1957.

This all started around 1948 when a former Japanese lieutenant colonel who had been attached to the General Staff Headquarters and was then running a secondhand clothes shop in the Shibuya area read an English letter from a US soldier to the Japanese woman with whom he was involved.

> Droves of other women who heard about this brought him "love letters" to translate, so eventually he opened an "English and French letter business". This continues to this day ten years later. Although business is not as good as it once was, two or three customers still come in every day. The fee is 150 yen per page. Given the nature of these letters, however, his business has ended up encompassing "love counselling" and "marriage counselling", and it is not unusual for him to spend half a day on a single letter. There are also quite a few letters about the procedures for getting married and about the birth of a baby or business negotiations. (*Yomiuri shimbun*, 23 November 1957)

In 1956 the price of a bread roll filled with red bean paste or jam was twelve yen (*Shukan Asahi*, ed., 1995: 16). These rolls now cost ten times that much, so the fee of 150 yen per page would be equivalent to about 1,500 yen today. This shop, where it was possible to communicate with an Occupation soldier for today's equivalent of 1,500 yen, was truly a contact zone where Occupation soldiers and Japanese women could interact. It is also noteworthy that the shop-owner who wrote the letters for these women had been a commissioned officer in the Imperial Army. What thoughts must have run through his head when Japanese women asked him to write love letters on their behalf to American soldiers, his former enemy?

Akio's book *Washinton Haitsu* (2011: 273–74) quotes an interview with the owner of the secondhand clothing shop that appeared in a booklet published by Shibuya ward in Tokyo, titled *Shibuya no ima* (Shibuya now). It offers additional insights to those in the *Yomiuri shimbun* article quoted above. The interview with the shop-owner reads as follows:

> When I write a love letter on behalf of a woman, I first make her spell out her goal. Money? Marriage? Enjoying the experience of being in love? Depending on the response, I work up a draft and suggest a strategy. By about 1965 nearly every woman was seeking marriage. Because all these women were serious-minded and earnest, many of them did end up happily married. (Akio 2011: 273)

The statement that 'By about 1965 nearly every woman was seeking marriage' implies that the earlier 'love letters' could be classified into three categories: money, marriage and love. As we have seen, however, it is difficult to draw lines between rape, sex work, love and marriage involving Occupation soldiers and Japanese women. For instance, Anne (who appeared in Chapter 6) was exclusively involved with the soldier who had raped her. The women who asked the owner of the secondhand clothing shop to write love letters on their behalf conceivably included some who, like Anne, were in a relationship with a soldier who had raped them. It is unclear how this businessman ended up reading 'foreign letters' to women involved with US soldiers, but at any rate the women had a former Japanese commissioned officer read their 'love letters' from Occupation soldiers who had served the enemy nation. This can be viewed as a survival strategy on the part of these women. Perhaps other women did the same after hearing rumors of this service.

This survival strategy is noteworthy. By having a Japanese man who had been a commissioned officer write 'love letters' on their behalf, the women maintained their connection with Occupation soldiers who had been repatriated. This was a survival strategy enacted by these women. Here the shop-owner played the role of an 'intermediary'. It is likely that similar 'love letter alleys' existed elsewhere around the country as a contact zone for maintaining communication with soldiers who had left Japan.

An examination of demographic factors allows us to infer that a considerable number of women experienced a romantic relationship with an Occupation soldier. By this I mean that the war deaths of Japanese men of marriageable age resulted in a limited pool of 'eligible' men available for women of marriageable age. This is illustrated by the figures presented in Table 7.1.

According to demographic statistics on the average marriage age each year and the age gap between husbands and wives as compiled by the Ministry of Health, Labour and Welfare in 2009, the average age for women marrying for the first time between 1947 and 1949 was around twenty-three, while for men it was around twenty-six. Keeping these ages in mind, let us look at the proportion of the population for each gender and age group in the different years in Table 7.1, based on the same source. Women aged between twenty and twenty-four in 1947 – a range that is relevant to the content of this book and includes the average age of women marrying

Table 7.1 Population by year, gender and age

Age	1935 (%)		1947 (%)		1950 (%)		1955 (%)	
	Women	Men	Women	Men	Women	Men	Women	Men
20–24	8.8	8.7	9.3	8.8	9.2	9.4	9.3	9.6
25–29	7.4	7.7	7.7	6.3	7.9	6.9	8.4	8.6
30–34	6.5	6.9	6.9	6.2	6.7	5.8	7.3	6.4
35–39	5.7	6.0	6.4	6.1	6.3	5.8	6.2	5.3
40–44	4.7	5.1	5.2	5.5	5.4	5.4	5.8	5.3

Note: Figures are rounded.
Source: Created by the author on the basis of the table in Ministry of Health, Labour and Welfare (2010), *Heisei 21 nen jinkodotaitokei kakuteisu jokan konin nenji sei nenreibetsu jinko* (Overview of 2009 official demographic statistics part 1: Married population by year, sex and age).

for the first time – accounted for 9.3 percent of the total population, an increase of 0.5 points since 1935. By contrast, the population of men aged between twenty-five and twenty-nine – a range that includes the average age of men marrying for the first time – shrank by 1.4 points. In 1935 the population of women aged between twenty and twenty-four stood at 3,034,288, but in 1947 that figure had risen to 3,699,448, an increase of 665,160. By contrast, in 1935 the population of men aged between twenty-five and twenty-nine stood at 2,670,248, but in 1947 it had dropped to 2,410,913, a decline of 259,335. In short, whereas between 1935 and 1947 the population of women aged between twenty and twenty-four had risen, the population of men aged between twenty-five and thirty-four had declined, presumably because they were killed in action. Meanwhile, because Japan's first marriage boom occurred in 1947–48 (Ministry of Health, Labour and Welfare 2017: 2), the number of 'eligible candidates' for women of marriageable age in 1947 was limited. Given these social circumstances, combined with the marriage boom, it is not surprising that some women experienced romance with Occupation soldiers.

The women whose relationships with Occupation soldiers did not lead to marriage were not in a position to speak openly of their romance in later years due to the stigma noted above. Being labeled a '*panpan*' not only involved discrimination in the form of being perceived as a woman who had a romantic entanglement with an Occupation soldier – i.e., as a prostitute who slept with someone from the victor's side – but was also compounded during the Occupation years by the stigma attached to unmarried women who lost their virginity and, for those who did not end up marrying the soldier, the stigma of having been 'abandoned' by a man. Hence the disrepute they suffered was far more severe than would have been the case today. Love with an Occupation soldier was associated with impurity, as seen in Takushi Crissey's (2017: 105) findings – in relation to the social stigma attached to unmarried women losing their virginity – that 'Any woman walking with an American soldier is seen as debased whether the woman is truly in love or just pretending to be in love to sell her body'. Drawing clear lines was difficult not only in the case of love, but also between the rape, sex work, love and marriage of women in relationships with Occupation soldiers. Nevertheless, as illustrated in this book, these women were lumped together as *panpan* and stigmatized accordingly. To understand just how problematic losing one's virginity before marriage was for women in those days, we simply need to recall the examples of Sakurako and Aoi, who were introduced earlier in this book. Both were victims who were raped by Occupation soldiers. Yet when they revealed to their father (Sakurako) and aunt (Aoi) that they had been raped, they were kicked out of home.

Because of the compound effect of these various stigmas, the women were unable to 'redefine their experience'

(Chizuko Ueno) in a self-affirming way by beginning to tell their own story.

Becoming able to reveal 'unacceptable' experiences

Kaori Hayashi (2002: 33) has raised the question of why Japanese war brides are associated with the image of prostitutes while European war brides are not. Is it really true that European war brides are not thought of in connection with sex work?

As mentioned earlier in this book, in liberated France there were women who at the time were contemptuously dubbed '*boniches*', a pejorative term for 'maid'. These were women who chose to become the lovers or 'fiancés' of US soldiers who arrived as liberators, and most of them came from 'good' families (Roberts 2013: 130–131). Given the existence of the pejorative term '*boniches*', it is difficult to believe that women who married soldiers from the liberation forces were not tainted by the image of prostitution, even if they were from good families. This is because they 'gave it up' to soldiers from the liberation forces.[4]

When Takushi Crissey went to Germany in 1994 to investigate American bases there, a female student at Bonn University whom she interviewed told her that 'The town of Giessen, where I grew up, is close to an American base. My mother said decent girls don't date American soldiers, and told me never to go out with them' (Takushi Crissey 2017: 124). Based on this statement, Takushi Crissey concluded that 'People in countries where foreign military forces are stationed tend to view them as a separate male group, and a negative attitude toward women who associate with them seems to be common throughout the world'.

Takushi Crissey's mention of this negative stance indicates that this phenomenon was not limited to Japan. 'Decent girls don't date American soldiers' is tantamount to saying that women who married American soldiers are not 'decent girls'. Hence it is difficult to conclude, as Hayashi did, that European war brides are *not* associated with the image of prostitutes in the case of marriage, which is an extension of dating.

Moreover, Takushi Crissey, who investigated testimonies held at the Boltzmann Institute in Salzburg, commented as follows about Austrian women who were in relationships with Occupation soldiers during the decade from 1945 during which US forces occupied Austria:

> The women who dated American soldiers were typists, waitresses, laundresses, and others who worked for the US military, as well as bar hostesses and prostitutes. Their motivations varied. Some were attracted to soldiers they thought were rich, and used sex to obtain material goods. Others fell in love and married. As for the soldiers, some started dating because they felt lonely stationed overseas, but later wanted to settle in Austria to be with the women they loved. The citizens of Salzburg aimed bitter hostility at these women, calling them "chocolate girls" and "Yankee wives" and claiming they besmirched Austrian honor. (Takushi Crissey 2017: 47)

This portrayal of Austrian women who dated Occupation soldiers as having 'besmirched Austrian honor' is identical to the situation of Japanese women who dated Occupation soldiers. Like Japanese women, these Austrians were 'women who slept with someone from the other side'. How on earth, then, would anyone conclude that European war brides are not symbolically associated with prostitution?[5]

At the very point where we ask whether war brides have a particular image – in this case, that of 'prostitute' – they become incapable of discussing any experiences other than those accepted by society. Even if their experiences were precious to them, as long as these are not accepted by society the women cannot speak of them.

Chapter 6 demonstrated through specific examples how not only is it difficult to distinguish between rape, prostitution, love and marriage when it comes to interactions between Occupation soldiers and women in occupied territories, but also how these experiences exist on a continuum of sexual violence. Being aware that war brides managed to somehow survive this situation while moving back and forth along this continuum allows them to speak of their experiences, which had slipped through the cracks of what is acceptable to society. At the same time, such an awareness is likely to serve as a catalyst for those women who did *not* end up marrying an Occupation soldier to begin sharing their experiences. This calls into question the attitude we adopt as we listen to these women's experiences.

Chapter 8

Children of the
Occupation

Single mothers raising children of the Occupation

Living under a false name and address

The case below involves a single mother who faced hardship immediately after her US soldier husband was killed in the war and she lost his support, even though she was legally married to him.

An *Asahi shimbun* article dated 29 November 1950 tells of the search by the family of a US soldier killed in action for the wife and son he left in Japan. According to the article, the husband was killed after his son was born, after which the mother and son moved houses and lived under different names. The actual report that the lost mother and child had been successfully located was welcome news, yet the mother's comment on her married life – 'I have fond memories of pleasant parties at clubs. The American ladies took my son under their wings' – suggests that she was compelled to change her name and relocate as soon as she lost the support of her husband. It is inconceivable that this would have happened to a single mother who had lost her Japanese husband. While the mother's family was not mentioned in the article, she probably did not have their backing, judging at least from the fact that she and her child took on different names.

This case indicates that single mothers of mixed-race children had to raise their offspring under harsher public scrutiny than did single mothers of Japanese children.

Aiming to raise 'ordinary Japanese'

On 1 February 1946, NHK (Japan Broadcasting Corporation) first broadcast an English conversation program, which gained instant popularity. Study groups for the 'Come, Come, Everybody' radio program were organized all over Japan, with some sending letters of gratitude to the instructor, Tadaichi Hirakawa (Taiheiyo Senso Kenkyukai, ed., 2006: 112). Young men and women lined up to snap up the American magazines *Life* and *Reader's Digest* on the days they went on sale (Harada 1994: 61). Post-war Japan saw an unprecedented boom in English conversation learning.

However, as mixed-blood children reached school age, an ironic twist was observed.

An article titled 'How mixed-blood children are accepted' (*Asahi shimbun*, 18 February 1954) tells the story of two sisters born to a Caucasian soldier and Japanese mother, Kurumi (alias). Kurumi lived with the soldier without being officially married to him and gave birth to two girls one year apart. After her 'husband' was killed in the Korean War, single mother Kurumi worked as a hostess at a cabaret frequented by sailors. The older girl was in the first year of elementary school, indicating that Kurumi had met and cohabited with her partner during the Occupation.

The ironic twist is that Kurumi gave up on having her daughters learn English, the language of their father, as the girls were bullied for being proud of having learned to read and write the alphabet. Kurumi decided to raise her daughters to be 'ordinary Japanese' so that they would not be picked on. While there were no issues with Japanese children learning English, mixed-blood children who learned English were targeted by bullies. For that reason, the mother gave up on her children's English education to raise them as 'ordinary Japanese'.

Mothers of mixed-blood children were thus implicitly expected to raise their children to behave even 'more Japanese' than ethnically Japanese children, so that they and their children could avoid friction with those around them.

American-style upbringing as a survival strategy for single mothers

When single mothers with mixed-blood children received no support from their families, they faced the twin hardships of earning a living and raising their children on their own, all while being subjected to public scrutiny. Out of the sixty-three women examined in this book, Matsuko (twenty-five) and Ruri (twenty) fall into this category.

Matsuko met an Occupation soldier at a cabaret where she was working. They moved in together and had a child. After that, she stayed in a relationship with him, receiving a monthly allowance of 25,000 yen, but apparently they did not continue to cohabit. Since the allowance was not sufficient to cover the high cost of hospital treatment for her VD as well as living expenses, Matsuko rented another place in which to entertain Occupation soldiers. She paid 3,000 yen a month for someone to look after her child, who was nineteen months old at the time. Matsuko's mother had died of an illness, but she still had her carpenter father, three older brothers, one younger brother and two younger sisters. The fact that she nevertheless left her child in another person's care indicates that she could not rely on her family. Her rent was high, and she spent as much as 5,000 yen (500,000 yen in current monetary values) per month on rice, charcoal and firewood. No small sum, this was comparable to the monthly salary of a rank-and-file soldier. Spending that much on those items suggests that for some reason Matsuko might not have had the identification papers needed to receive rations. She had to earn a living and raise her child all by herself.

While the Introduction discussed the monthly salaries of Allied soldiers, let us take a closer look at their salaries and those of the Japanese. Twenty-five-year-old John D. Grisman, MD, a commissioned officer who was appointed as the head of the Public Health Section of the Kyoto Military Government Team in September 1947, received a monthly salary of US$160, while rank-and-file soldiers earned US$20 a month (Nishimura 2015: 42). If Grisman's salary remained the same in 1948, he would have earned the equivalent of 43,200 yen (based on the rate of 1 USD = 270 JPY), while a rank-and-file soldier's monthly salary would have been 5,400 yen. In 1948, an elementary school teacher's starting pay was 2,000 yen per month, and in 2015 it stood at 201,900 yen. Based on these figures, Grisman and a rank-and-file soldier respectively made 4,320,000 yen and 540,000 yen per month in current currency values. Even a young Allied soldier earned more than twice as much as a new Japanese teacher.

Among the sixty-three women, Kasumi (age unknown) and Yuri (twenty; discussed in Chapter 5) disclosed their fathers' monthly income. Kasumi's father worked at a central wholesale market and earned 4,000 to 5,000 per month, while Yuri's father was a railroad man with a monthly income of about 10,000 yen.

Streetwalkers investigated the income of 195 women in their previous employment (Takenaka and Sumiya, eds., 1949: 143–147). According to this survey, the average monthly incomes, at shops or companies run by Japanese, were 8,812 yen for dancers, 2,237 yen for office workers[1] and 878 yen for factory workers, with dancers topping the list. Judging from their higher income, the dancers' clientele would have been Occupation soldiers.

When they worked at US military bases, however, women's average monthly income would more than double. The highest earners were *shakufu shogi* (barmaids / sex workers), with an average income of 7,425 yen per month. Occupation forces' 'comfort facilities' had been closed prior to this and *shakufu shogi* were not supposed to exist, yet they operated unofficially. One of the sixty-three women, eighteen-year-old Sara, said she earned money from dressmaking in the daytime and from 'attending banquets' at night. Her income was 12,000 yen per month (500 yen from dressmaking), with her night-time earnings exceeding women's average monthly income, which suggests that she worked as a *shakufu shogi* for Occupation soldiers.

The second-highest earners were office workers (typists), housemaids, shop assistants and hospitality workers, who made 4,054 yen per month on average. Housekeepers earned more money than housemaids due to their role supervising the household, with some making as much as 15,000 yen per month. Next in line were café waitresses, with an average monthly income of 3,300 yen.

Keeping these figures in mind, let us return to the case of Matsuko. She paid 3,000 yen per month to leave her child in someone's care. 'I also constantly need to buy my kid such things as snacks', she said. The childcare cost of 3,000 yen is comparable to the monthly income of a maid working in an Occupation officer's household. Four of the sixty-three women previously worked as housemaids. Three of them had completed at least girls' high school; one of the three graduated from a women's college and had worked as a housekeeper. In those days, girls' schools sometimes placed their graduates in housemaid jobs. A single mother whose husband died of an illness worked as a maid and babysitter at an MP's house; the wife of her former teacher at a girls' high school introduced her to this job. Home parties were often held at the MP's place, which was 'a completely different world from Japanese people's lives at that time' (Nara no Josei Seikatsu-shi Hensan Iinkai [Editorial committee of Nara Women's Lives], ed., 1995: 483–484). This case shows that women of good background with a girls' high school education were selected to care for the children of officer-class families.

Matsuko seems to have engaged a housemaid/nanny who would more likely have worked in the household of an Occupation officer rather than as a nanny for a Japanese family.

Ruri was not interested in studying, so she dropped out of girls' high school and ran away from home. After becoming pregnant to her Occupation soldier boyfriend, she returned to her parents' home. Both parents were alive, with her father employed at a rubber company. Ruri explains: 'My family had no idea of how I lived. But I had to return home because I fell pregnant. My parents were fiercely opposed [to my having a child] ([…] their thinking was that if the father were Japanese, things could be managed somehow or another, but not so with a mixed-blood child), so now I just live with my child'. Ruri could not rely on her parents for help, so she paid 3,000 yen per month to hire a nanny. This cost for childcare suggests that the person she engaged was on the level of a maid working in an Occupation officer's household.

The cases of Matsuko and Ruri reveal that they spent a considerable sum on their children's upbringing – all the more significant because of their status as single mothers with no family support. It is assumed that they engaged someone with experience as a maid in an officer's household so that their children could become 'the children of the occupier' through an American-style upbringing and they could become 'the mother of the occupier's children'. This was the survival strategy adopted by Matsuko and Ruri, who faced not only discrimination against their mixed-blood children but also social prejudice against single mothers. Neither had any choice but to bring up their child on their own without any family support.

Single mothers of 'black' Japanese children

Statistics on mixed-blood children: 'yellow' children excluded by Ministry of Health and Welfare

The results of a survey on mixed-blood children conducted by the Ministry of Health and Welfare appeared in a *Mainichi shimbun* article on 5 May 1953. The numbers of mixed-blood children were as follows: 3,004 of white descent (*hakujin-kei*), 400 of black descent (*kokujin-kei*) and eighty-six of unclear descent. Kano (2007: 239) points out that the ministry focused only on 'black' and 'white' origins in its survey on so-called mixed-blood children,[2] with children of 'yellow descent' (*oshoku-kei*) not covered by the survey. Let us look at the *Mainichi* article in more detail, keeping in mind that children of 'yellow descent' were not included. Eighty-four percent of the fathers had US nationality, followed by Australian, Filipino and British. Sixty-two per cent of the children were acknowledged by their fathers, while the remaining fathers were unknown. The financial burden of raising the children was largely borne by the mothers, with only two biological fathers providing responsible childcare support. The children in the survey were predominantly of white descent: eighty-six per cent of the 3,490 children had white fathers while thirteen percent were of black descent. Even considering that fewer black soldiers were in Japan, these figures suggest that more pregnancies of 'black' children might have been terminated. The number of children born to Nikkei soldiers and how they were treated are unknown. Further research is needed on the experiences of Nikkei fathers' children and the children's mothers.

'I'm not coming home tonight': survival strategies of mothers who cannot come home

There were some cases in which children of white descent were looked after by their maternal grandparents. Hana, the mother of 'a cute child, with [REDACTED] eyes', referred to in Chapter 4, worked in Kyoto, leaving her child in the care of her mother in Kumamoto. Kurumi's daughters, referred to at the beginning of this chapter, were looked after by her father. We might infer that 'Caucasian descent' was

Photo 8.1 A back view of Charlie (eleven) and Machiko (seven) walking hand in hand

possibly a major reason why Hana and Kurumi were able to leave their children in their parents' care. What about the mothers of children born to black soldiers?

Photo 8.1 shows the front cover image of my earlier work *Who Were Panpan?*. This image, showing a back view of Charlie (eleven) and Machiko (seven) walking hand in hand, originally appeared in the article 'Abandoned mixed-blood children' (4 August 1957, *Asahi Graph*, nos. 8 and 9). They were fathered by an African-American sergeant who was posted to Japan just after the war ended, while their mother Hasu (alias) was Japanese. The father had returned to the US two years earlier and had been out of contact since then. Hasu raised her children while working at a foreigners-only bar. She told the reporter that while in Kobe she was a victim of the war and the end of the war saw her family break up. She met the sergeant while she was selling goods on the black market to Occupation soldiers. Charlie was born soon after, and their relationship continued for nine years until the father returned to the US. It appears that on several occasions he filed an application for an extension of stay so as to maintain their family relationship. According to Kaori Miyanishi, who conducted research on Japanese wives at the US Marine Corps Base by volunteering on the front desk at the Personal Service Center in Camp Foster (Camp Zukeran) in Okinawa from October 2005, US military personnel usually move every three years, and often they are deployed to war for an extended period or ordered to leave Okinawa for training (Miyanishi 2012: 9). Miyanishi explains that military personnel's lives involve moving beyond the social space of Okinawa, which can put strain on their relationships and cause friction and marital breakdown. In the case of Asa in Chapter 4 of this volume, her second partner applied to extend his posting for another three years when ordered to return home. Hence it is possible that Occupation soldiers were also relocated every three years. As they lived a 'life on the move', their relationship with Japanese women was also incorporated in this cycle of relocation.

Tamura (2002: 153) notes that many Japanese women were left in Japan even though they had been romantically involved with Australian soldiers, while Shigeyoshi Yasutomi (2005a: 37), who researches Japanese-Americans, cautions that we must remember that many relationships did not result in marriage for various reasons and that those Japanese women were unable to cross the ocean. Thus, many were left behind in Japan when their close relationship with an Occupation soldier did not lead to marriage.

Of the sixty-three women examined in this book, nineteen broke up with their partners when the men were ordered to return home. In other words, return orders triggered separations for one-third of the women.

Twenty-one-year-old Ai met a telegraph and electrical engineer when she worked as a typist at a US military base in Fukuoka, and the two moved in together. When the engineer was transferred to Kyoto, she relocated with him. However, judging from Ai's comment that 'When the time comes to part from W, I'll live independently', she continued the relationship while mentally preparing for the fact that 'his returning home means breaking up'. Nineteen-year-old Natsume was in contact with her partner's family back home and had expressed her desire to marry him, but she was concerned whether this was possible given the international circumstances of the day. Twenty-year-old Yuzu, who jointly owned a property in Osaka with her partner, likewise wished to marry him but was worried about what would happen after he returned home.

As seen above, return orders were the greatest concern for women in relationships with Occupation soldiers. It is clear that Charlie and Machiko's father, who did not immediately return home when initially ordered to do so and stayed on in Kobe for nine years, can be regarded as a man with a degree of integrity. At the same time, he did not legally marry Charlie and Machiko's mother despite spending nine years with them; he eventually went home and lost contact. In the end, he abandoned his partner and children after nine years.

Hasu, however, never abandoned her children, yet the title of the abovementioned article describes Charlie and Machiko as 'abandoned mixed-blood children'. The article implies at times that the reporter regarded Hasu as a mother who neglected her children. The caption for Photo 8.1 says: 'When the neon lights turn on, the children come to a bar district frequented by foreigners and follow foreigners around. Some give money to the children, but it seems they are not here only for money. The "blood" in their veins probably prompts them to come here in search of the same blood'.

It is true that their US solider father's blood flows through Charlie and Machiko's veins. Yet it is pure speculation on the reporter's part that the reason the children 'come to a bar district frequented by foreigners' is that they are 'in search of the same blood'. The main text states that 'Their mother works at a foreigners-only bar and tends to be away overnight. Charlie-kun and Machiko-chan rove the streets every day and night. Those who use Motomachi Station in Kobe would have seen this wretched brother and sister more than once'. The article concludes: 'There are around 4,000 "mixed-blood" war babies in Japan (Ministry of Health and Welfare survey), and with the reported major withdrawal of Occupation forces the misery experienced by Charlie-kun and Machiko-chan will be repeated somewhere in Japan'. The article overemphasizes the 'misery' of Charlie and Machiko as black mixed-blood children – abandoned by not only their father but also their mother.

Let us now discuss their mother, Hasu. The article critically notes, 'She goes off to work sourly saying "Why do Japanese bully my children?". She will not come home tonight yet again'. Hasu knew that Charlie and Machiko were bullied, and her reference to 'Japanese' suggests that it was not just other children who bullied them. We can tell from the children's clothes that Hasu cared for them. While the family lived in a shack without electricity, the children were dressed neatly. Photo 8.1 shows Machiko wearing a gingham dress and sporting a hair accessory that might be hard to make out in the image. In another photo Machiko has her hair tied in two ponytails with ribbons, and yet another shows Charlie wearing a neat sleeveless V-necked shirt. Hasu supported her family by working at a foreigners-only bar, but their living standards had fallen greatly after the children's father left. This highlights the struggles of a single mother who had lost her GI partner. The fact that Hasu was often away overnight was simply because she needed money for her 'black' children to live as comfortably as possible in Japanese society. Even though she looked after her children as best she could while barely making ends meet, in the article there is not a word of appreciation for her efforts. Moreover, her existence as a struggling single mother seems to have been erased. Not coming home at night was part of Hasu's survival strategy to desperately defend life with her children, to the extent that she was not *able* to come home.

At that time mixed-blood children were everywhere.[3] Nevertheless, Charlie and Machiko were featured in the magazine as 'abandoned mixed-blood children'. This was not only because Hasu did not have her family's support but also because she had 'black' Japanese children, who accounted for only thirteen percent of interracial children. Furthermore, her partner, the father of her children, had left Japan. For those reasons, the reporter wrote this article in a negative way that implicitly condemned the mother by sympathizing with her children. If the children's father had been white, they might not have been featured in this way. How they were treated in the magazine partially reveals the social circumstances that surrounded the mothers of 'black' children.

Differences in the status of mixed-blood children and their mothers

Harsh scrutiny of mothers who had mixed-blood children outside 'legitimate marriage'

Although mixed-blood children and their mothers both had relationships with Occupation solders, their positions were completely different, because the mothers 'voluntarily' established intimate relationships with the soldiers. A 'Tensei jingo' (vox populi, vox Dei) column in *Asahi shimbun* dated 11 July 1952 clearly shows the difference in their status. While the statement that 'children are not to be blamed' appears twice, the article describes their mothers as 'slutty Yamato Nadeshiko' (loose women who have abandoned the traditional virtues). The writer assumes that mixed-blood children were born 'outside of proper marriage and often from prostitution'. We must remember however, that Japan was under an occupation in which the masculinized victor dominated the feminized defeated.

In this unequal power relationship, some Japanese women gave birth to mixed-blood children through unwanted pregnancies, including those that resulted from rape. Nevertheless, from the viewpoint of the author of the 'Tensei jingo' column, mothers of mixed-blood children were either legitimately married women or prostitutes.

Kurumi, discussed earlier in this chapter, said 'I think most mothers of mixed-blood children are like me and are suffering the same pain'. Her de-facto GI partner was killed in war, and she was raising her two daughters by working as a hostess at a cabaret frequented by sailors. She said she felt distressed about her daughters' increasing awareness of gossip about her past and her work as they got older. Such phrases as 'I'm *ainoko* [a crossbreed]' and 'Mom, you must have money because you're in a good line of business' came out of her daughters' mouths. 'Who would say such things to my daughters?', Kurumi wondered.

Such expressions as '*ainoko*' and 'good line of business' clearly indicate that people around them regarded Kurumi, with her mixed-blood children, as a *panpan*. This view of such mothers is shared by the author of the 'Tensei jingo' column.

A middle school (junior high) girl's 'premonition of violence'

Unlike mothers of mixed-blood children, children are not 'voluntarily' born of mixed-blood, as they cannot choose their parents. The book *Kichi no ko* (Base children) referred to in Chapter 7 includes seven essays titled 'Poor mixed-blood children' written by elementary and middle school students. Two essays describe the increase in mixed-blood children as problematic (third-year middle school student [male] in Yokohama and third-year middle school student [male] in Aomori prefecture); four essays 'feel sorry' for these children's situation and directly or indirectly criticize their mothers (fifth-year elementary school student [female] in Tottori prefecture; second-year middle school student [female] in Shizuoka prefecture; third-year middle school student [female] in Tachikawa; second-year middle school student [female] in Kure). Only one essay written by a female student in the third year of middle school in Aomori prefecture offers a different perspective. While this essay shares with the other four a sentiment of pity toward mixed-blood children, it differs in that it criticizes only the American soldiers who fathered them. The short piece titled 'Children with tainted blood' reads as follows:

When American forces finish their military exercises

Soldiers give children chewing gum and pocket change

And look for the whereabouts of *ojosan* [young ladies]

That would be all there is to it, I thought

But they taint blood

And make women give birth to babies

I feel sorry for those babies

The Japan Association for the Protection of Children and the Japan Teachers' Union co-organized the National Conference on Protecting Military Base Children in March 1953 in Yokosuka. The book *Kichi Nihon* (Base Japan), edited by Kozo Inomata, Kihachiro Kimura and Ikutaro Shimizu (1953), was one outcome of the conference. Part 1 focuses on 'The alarming situation with military bases: on-site reportage', with reports from local elementary and middle school teachers from all over Japan except for Okinawa. A report by middle school teacher Goro Senba in Aomori draws on police data to reveal that there was a sizable number of streetwalkers in Hachinohe near the US Misawa Base. He also notes that in the town of Misawa cheap houses were hastily constructed one after another to house Japanese women with a clientele of American soldiers (Senba 1953: 26). Pimps were always loitering around these bases. Yet we can see from the composition by the third-year middle school student that some soldiers looked for young women – the kind of women the children regarded as '*ojosan*' – not through pimps but with the help of village children by giving them 'chewing gum and pocket change'. Those soldiers were clearly after young women who were not prostitutes by trade. We might even say that the children who introduced '*ojosan*' to US soldiers inadvertently played the role of 'intermediaries' for the soldiers and '*ojosan*'.

The expression 'That would be all there is to it, I thought' indicates that what actually happened was more than just those soldiers 'meeting' *ojosan*. They 'made them give birth to babies', with this coercive-sounding expression suggestive of unwanted pregnancies which would have included those that resulted from rape. Consequently, it is conceivable that the girl's expression 'they taint blood' implies more than what Kano (2007: 241) describes as 'the perception of children who took *konketsu* [mixed-blood] literally'. The student who wrote it lived in a village. Everyone in the village knew about the women who gave birth to these children, and the student would also have known or heard about them. The mention of American forces suggests that multiple soldiers were involved. While mixed-blood children were a taboo topic during the Occupation, the end of the Occupation coincided with these children reaching school age, which prompted a surge in media coverage of them in 'independent' Japan. Like the other essays, this piece expresses sympathy toward mixed-blood children but does not seem to show any sympathy for their mothers. Nevertheless, while the tone of much writing is unilaterally critical of the mothers, this text by a female middle school student offers an important perspective that sheds light on the existence of *ojosan* who gave birth after unwanted pregnancies.

Ichiro Tomiyama, a historian of early modern and modern Okinawa, uses the expression 'premonition of violence' (2002) to describe a 'sense of danger' that is not immediately relevant in one's everyday life but is no longer completely irrelevant (Tomiyama 2013: 15). Given the age of the third-year middle school student, we might argue that she somehow had a 'premonition of violence' – that she herself was concerned she might be subjected to incomprehensible sexual violence in the form of rape by American soldiers. The 'premonition of violence' she experienced was not only that of actual violence perpetrated by a US solider but also a premonition of 'second rape' in the form of gossip among the locals. We should note that, as revealed by this composition, there were some women who felt a 'premonition of violence' in their daily lives around military bases.

Different attitudes toward 'Boche babies' and '*panpan* babies'

'Boche babies' who redefined their experiences

Bearing in mind that mixed-blood children and their mothers were regarded differently, let us now compare the situation of children of the occupations in France and Japan. While stigmatized children born in German-occupied France have been able to redefine their experiences in a self-affirming manner by reframing their past, which they had sealed away for over six decades, children of *panpan* are yet to do so. Here we investigate why some mixed-blood children have been able to define their experiences while others have not.

A good example of positive cases is 'Boche babies',[4] a derogatory term used for children born to occupying German soldiers and French women during World War II.

Let us focus on Josiane Kruger, who was born to a German soldier and a French mother. In her autobiography *Les embryons de guerre* (The embryos of war),[5] published in 2006, Kruger recalls how shocked she was when her elementary school classmate called her 'Boche baby' in the schoolyard during break.

Despite feeling intimidated, I went up to a group of kids to whom my friend who sat next to me in class belonged. A big girl flashed me a scornful glance and shouted: "go away, you Boche baby!"

I still remember the intense shock I felt. It was the first time I'd been called "Boche baby", and I didn't understand what it signified. On my return home that day I put my bag on the table, calmed myself down, and then asked my mother.

"Maman, what does boche mean?" My mother had not even been aware I was back home, possibly because she was irritated about the tricky task of making some gloves. As shocked by my words as if she had been electrocuted, she cried out with a strained expression on her face.

"Why do you ask such a thing!"

"Everybody at school calls me 'Boche baby'", I responded with downcast eyes. My mother gave me a penetrating stare with her intense blue eyes, a stare that seemed to pierce my retina. (Kruger 2007: 22–24)[6]

Kruger's autobiography was self-published in France in 2006. Another autobiography titled *Orgueilleuse* (Proud) was first published in 2004 by Suzanne Lardreau, who from the age of four mostly grew up in an orphanage at a convent where she was treated with contempt by the nuns and the convent's cooks. She also redefined her experiences by narrating her own story (2010: 248), writing that 'girls with clipped hair' are no longer defective, and that they share a particularity spawned by history. In this way, after the elapse of over six decades, stigmatized children of the Boche have started to redefine their experiences.

The ability to do so stemmed from the impact generated by a documentary film on this topic titled *Enfants de Boches*

(Children of the Boche), which first aired on television channel France 3 in 2002 (rebroadcast in 2003).[7] Another documentary, titled *Passé sous silence* (The past hidden in silence), which was broadcast in 2005, also addressed the topic of Boche babies. Kruger explains that many of those who watched the two documentaries resolved to come out from the darkness into the light for the first time (2007: 117). She further describes how the fact that she was born to a German soldier and a French woman was suppressed by silence and had always haunted her in the form of excruciating emotional distress (2007: 182). This distress stemmed from the fact that these children suffered from the contempt of others, because romantic relationships between French women and occupying German soldiers were regarded as treacherous acts and as collaboration after the German military administration ended. In 2005, the French National Association of War Children (ANEG) was established, and Kruger is now a spokesperson for the association. She says: 'While listening to people and disseminating information in my role as a spokesperson, I feel we have come to wish to be released from our past and to find our origins'. Coming face to face with her own roots, Kruger realized that each child had shut themselves up in their own tragedy based on a sense of shame and helplessness and had lived under the belief that they were alone in this situation (2007: 184–185). Having been a Boche baby herself, Kruger's own memories are being freed by working through her past and listening to others and disseminating information as an ANEG spokesperson.

In April 2005, about 100 men and women from all over France gathered in the boarding area in an airport bound for Berlin, in the hope of finding out about the fathers they had never known and any surviving family members they might meet. These people were among an estimated 200,000 children born to occupying German soldiers and French women during the war. This was recorded as part of a documentary broadcast on 6 May 2005.

> When we arrived at the boarding area, no one knew each other. But as we started talking, we opened up to one another. Using familiar appellations and calling each other by our first names just like old friends, we had so much to talk about. Even after arriving at the hotel in Berlin, we gathered in small groups and kept chatting away with no signs of stopping. Each of us told about ourselves and asked about the others, and it was as if this endless loop of conversation took away all the anguish we had lived through for decades. (Kruger 2007: 177–178)

The above process of releasing memories is similar to that experienced by the victims of sexual violence perpetrated by Japanese forces in Shanxi province, China. Historian Yoneko Ishida, who interviewed female victims and supported their court cases, explains how suppressed memories are released, based on her understanding that evolved through repeated interviews.

> The women narrated their painful experiences again and again and listened to what other women went through while staying at the same place together and sometimes getting into arguments. As this went on, they recalled things they had forgotten or didn't want to remember. When we asked them if they knew about certain incidents, they would later ask their grandfathers about it. Consequently, they became aware of what had happened in their village, things they didn't know about. Those interactions were video-recorded and edited for a wider Japanese audience. The women

came to gatherings of Japanese to view the edited recordings. While they didn't understand Japanese, they intently watched the videos in which they featured. This allowed them to contextualize what had happened to them within the broader framework of the harm done to their village as a whole. In the course of realizing there were people who empathized with their sufferings enough to become angry and to shed tears with them, they grew to recognize what had happened to them. A grievous wrong ruined each woman's life, but through interacting with others they were able to recognize that this wasn't a personal issue restricted to a single person. When the past they had wanted to forget was narrativized, the women came face to face with what had happened and were able to gradually heal. Contact with Japanese people who shed tears at these women's stories was also important.[8] (Ishida 2002: 25–26)

Referring to Christophe Weber's documentary film *Enfants de Boches*, Kruger notes that Weber's work served to connect many people who were searching for their origins (2007: 177). Caring and empathetic listeners are essential for narrators to verbalize their traumatized and stigmatized experiences (Ueno, Araragi and Hirai, eds., 2018: xii). Children of the Boche were able to redefine their experiences because of the 'attentive and empathetic' listener, Christophe Weber. In the case of Kruger, her activities as a spokesperson of ANEG also facilitated the process of releasing the memories of her secretive past and finding her origins.

Panpan babies who cannot redefine their experiences

Children born to Occupation soldiers and Japanese women have been generally regarded as '*panpan* babies'. An essay by a third-year elementary school student who was called a *panpan* baby is included in the abovementioned *Kichi no ko* anthology.

> Back in the day when my father was in Japan, he cuddled me on his lap, bought me pretty dresses and gave me chocolate, saying "Come on, eat up now". Those were the good days, but after he went back to America, sad things keep happening to me. My father sometimes sends money from America, but my mother soon spends it all. […] My first father went to Korea. That was years ago, and he hasn't come back. My mother doesn't really tell me how my second father is doing in America. My friend called me a "*panpan* baby", and I cried. I went to tell my teacher. The teacher talked to my friend. Then my friend stopped calling me "*panpan* baby". […] I wonder if my mother was a *panpan*. I don't know. (Shimizu, Miyahara and Ueda, eds., 1953: 157–159)

The student who wrote this essay, Madoka (alias), seems to have had two non-Japanese 'fathers'. The father who went to Korea was presumably deployed to the Korean front. Madoka's mother Kana (alias) worked at a noodle shop near a station. Madoka was left in the care of an *obasan* (aunt or carer) and did not live with Kana. The fact that Madoka's friend called her a *panpan* baby suggests that her classmates' parents shared the view that Kana, who was in an intimate relationship with an American man but was not married to him, was a *panpan* and that her daughter Madoka was a *panpan* baby. That view would also have been widespread among the children at school.

Let us now discuss Kana. The essay was written during the two-month period around 26 November 1952 (Shimizu,

Miyahara and Ueda, eds., 1953: 328), which indicates that Madoka, who was then in the third year of elementary school, was born in 1943 and that her biological father could not have been the father who went to Korea or the second American father.

This means that, for some reason or another, Kana and Madoka were living by themselves just after the war. Kana might have severed her ties with her family or lost her parents and other family members in the war. In any case, it seems that this mother and child did not have any family they could rely on after the war ended. Those were probably the circumstances under which Kana entered a relationship with the man who went to Korea; she found a man who knew she had a daughter and who could be Madoka's 'father'. This was Kana's survival strategy for raising her daughter. Madoka describes her fond memories of the father who returned to the US, but she hardly mentions the father who went to Korea, which suggests that she preferred the second man. He must also have cared about Kana and Madoka, as he sent them money from time to time. Kana survived the postwar period with Madoka by strategically getting into relationships with two foreigners who had some financial resources. Here again, we see the situation of single mothers who lack family support. Given that Madoka wrote 'I can say anything to my teacher', it seems that her schoolteacher (a woman) was the only outsider who had shown empathy toward her. The teacher apparently understood that Kana had been in a relationship with an American and was singlehandedly raising Madoka after he returned home.

The critical difference from German-occupied France is that women in Japan who had relationships with Occupation soldiers without formally getting married were unilaterally stigmatized. Possible reasons include the difference in position between the fathers of Boche babies and *panpan* babies. German soldiers were on the defeated side that retreated from France, so Boche babies were the children of the defeated. By contrast, the Occupation forces in Japan were the victor, making *panpan* babies the children of the victor. In other words, when Germany was defeated, French women who had intimate relationships with German soldiers transitioned from 'women defecting to the victor's side' into 'women involved with the defeated side'. Precisely because their lovers fell from the victor's position to that of the defeated, women who had 'defected to the victor's side' were harshly punished by having their heads shaved in public. Japanese women who had a liaison with Occupation soldiers, 'the victor', did not receive such severe treatment.

If, along the lines of Boche babies, the notion of Yankee babies had existed in reference to children born to Occupation soldiers and Japanese women, how Yankee babies' experiences would have been redefined would have differed from the situation with *panpan* babies. Children born of a legal marriage with soldiers on the victor's side are able to walk tall in society. However, the children of unmarried mothers were not regarded as children of the victor; instead, they were an object of contempt as 'the children of women who were dumped by the victor'. That is why they remain the children of *panpan*, not Yankee children. It is therefore critically important that these children are allowed to redefine their experiences so as to affirm their identities by relating their own stories as the children of *panpan*.

How can women recount and redefine their experiences?

As long as 'not being a *panpan*' is the condition for women's narratives of their romantic relationships (with Occupation soldiers) to be socially accepted, those whose relationships did not result in marriage cannot talk about their former partners. This is because 'conditions that enable discourse also act to allow specific discourses but suppress others' (Ueno 2018: 5). As mentioned in Chapter 7, when women speak of their romantic relationships with Occupation soldiers that did not result in marriage, they become stigmatized as 'former *panpan*'. The stigma connotes 'women who defected to the victor's side', 'discrimination against prostitutes', and 'unmarried women' losing their chastity, as well as 'women who were dumped by the victor'. Since women who were dumped by the victor are no longer 'women on the victor's side', Japanese people's rancor toward the victor is relentlessly directed at these women. The term '*panpan*' involves an intricately entangled web of multi-layered discrimination. As a result, the children of *panpan* are perceived by society as the children of women dumped by the victor.

For women who did not end up marrying their soldier-partner to talk freely about their romantic relationship, they need 'caring and empathetic listeners'. As researchers who study women who were romantically involved with soldiers, we are also responsible for the lack of such listeners. When these women have 'caring and empathetic' listeners like Christophe Weber in relation to Boche babies and Yoneko Ishida in relation to the victims of sexual violence perpetrated by the Japanese army in Shanxi province, they will finally be able to redefine their experiences. The presence of such listeners will also enable the children of *panpan* to redefine *their* experiences. These possibilities act as a catalyst for change in community perceptions toward those women, and allows women who married Occupation soldiers to redefine their experiences anew without suppressing others' narratives.

Over seventy years have passed since the end of the war. The number of women who had intimate relationships with Occupation soldiers and who may be able to redefine their experiences is rapidly diminishing. Therefore, recognizing the various survival strategies adopted by the women who were called *panpan* is a matter of urgency. This is also vital for restoring the honor of those who have passed away without their experiences being redefined.

Lastly, I would like to reiterate that the women who were called *panpan* survived the two major hardships of Japan's defeat in the war and its subsequent occupation. I would also like to emphasize that their strategies and agency were practical means of survival for them as victims who were exposed to the crushing violence of the Occupation.

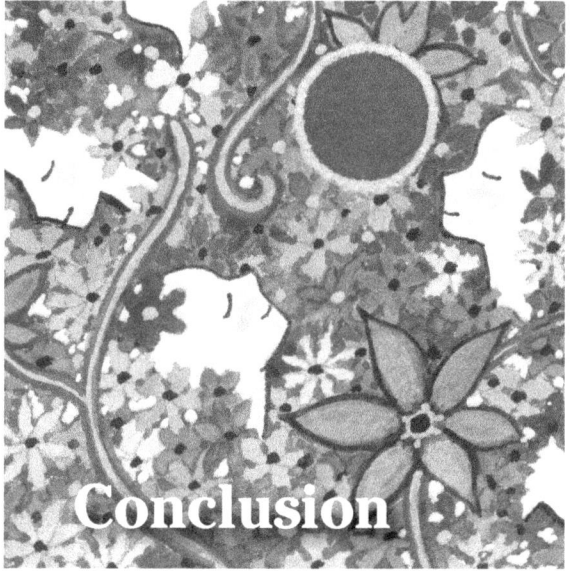

Conclusion

Women and Soldiers

The sexual violence of compulsory VD screening: a history that cannot be erased

In the 21 January 2017 issue of the Japanese edition of the Korean newspaper *The Hankyoreh*, there was an article titled 'State must compensate "comfort women" in US military base towns'. The news came as I was writing this book. To start with the result, the court delivered a verdict that the state (Korea) must compensate for the damage inflicted upon the 'comfort women' plaintiffs working at the US military base towns. The court found that it was illegal for the state to enforce the internment of these women into quarantine facilities for Venereal Disease Control (VDC). Moreover, it found that the state was liable for compensating fifty-seven victims of the US 'comfort women' scheme who were put into isolation at hospitals specializing in VDs prior to August 1977, when the enforcement regulations clarifying which VDs would be targeted were established.[1] If we look at this verdict in the context of Japan during the Occupation, it would mean that the false arrests and detention of women in hospitals fenced by barbed wire, which occurred in Japan before the promulgation of the Venereal Disease Prevention Law on 15 July 1948, were illegal.

Needless to say, the Korean verdict was groundbreaking in itself, but it was equally so in that the women in the US camp towns sued the state. Regrettably, this would be unthinkable in present-day Japan. As I have already explained in detail in my previous book, *Who Were Panpan?*, the women detained in these VD hospitals were treated like criminals rather than patients.[2] Even today, few people in Japanese society are aware of the false arrests and forced VD screenings during the Occupation era.

There used to be several municipal hospitals in Kobe City that specialized in VDs. One was Kobe City Higashiyama Hospital (hereafter Higashiyama Hospital). It was a general hospital that treated various infectious diseases, including VDs. *Higashiyama Byoin shi* (History of Higashiyama Hospital; exec. ed. Hori, ed. Sato, 1956) describes the history of the hospital from 1889 (Meiji 22) to 1956 (Showa 31), compressing each decade into just four pages. Chapter 5 (1945–1954), which covers the Occupation period, includes descriptions, some as brief as one line, of diseases such as typhoid fever, diphtheria, dysentery, cholera and Japanese encephalitis. One example notes that 'As a quarantine measure, in view of last year's severe typhus epidemic, the US Occupation forces carried out a thorough extermination of lice targeting homeless and other people under GHQ's strict orders, by mass widespread spraying of DDT'. Not a word is mentioned in the hospital history, however, about VDC during the Occupation. During this period, arrest vans akin to those pursuing stray dogs were driven all over Japan, and Kobe was no exception.

Hyogo prefecture, where Kobe is located, submitted an application for a national subsidy for VD prevention to the Minister of Health and Welfare on 1 March 1949. According to national funding records for the fiscal year 1949, published in 1950 by the General Affairs section of the Hyogo Prefecture Hygiene Department, grant applications were made to cover VD hospital costs, compulsory health examinations, investigations into contact persons, treatment of VDs, public relations costs and consigned hospitalization costs. Here, 'compulsory health examinations' refers to mandatory VD screenings. What this document shows is the fact that mandatory examinations were carried out by the state under the name of 'compulsory health examinations'.

Despite this, there is no mention of VDs in the official history of the hospital. As confirmed in *Hyogo: Fusetsu nijunen* (Hyogo: A twenty-year ordeal), 'those with venereal diseases were forcibly admitted to the detention center on level four of the Higashiyama Hospital' (Iwasa 1966: 155), the ward specializing in VDs. The fact that Iwasa uses the expression 'forcibly admitted to the detention center' indicates that, as in Korea, specialist hospitals for VDs were in fact detention facilities in occupied Japan. Iwasa, a newspaper journalist, must have actually visited the hospital. Furthermore, Miyoshi Miyazaki (then an elementary school student), who was receiving treatment at the hospital around this time for a different infectious disease, also confirmed that there was a VD ward in Higashiyama Hospital.

Concealing the fact that VDs were treated during the Occupation period is an act of erasure by those in power of the oppression and coercion of Japanese women in the contact zones, the meeting places where Japanese women met the Occupation soldiers with whom they would form intimate relationships. Moreover, it is an attempt to erase all traces of resistance and negotiation by women against such oppression and coercion. In the end, this meant that the concealment extended to everything related to VD treatment, including abortion, childbirth, adoption and so on. Unlike typhoid, diphtheria, dysentery, cholera and Japanese encephalitis, VD examinations and treatment were forced upon any woman of the occupied territories suspected by the authorities of having had sexual relations with members of the occupying forces. Documenting these details, from the perspective of hospitals in defeated Japan, would have amounted to leaving a record of the 'dishonorable' history of being forced to examine and treat women who were 'prostitutes' working for the occupying forces who were viewed as 'women who had deserted to the enemy'. It seems likely that this might be the reason for the failure to include the records of these women's examinations and treatment in the history of the hospital. Needless to say, the erasure constitutes nothing less than crossing out the record of abuse committed against Japanese women during the Occupation.

The removal of the treatment record from the hospital's history also means the erasure of the fact that these women were forced to go through intimate examinations with or without their consent in order to find out whether they had VDs. Using a point raised by Diet member Michiko Fujiwara, historian Kazuko Hirai states how sexually violent these examinations were. Describing an incident in Gotenba, in which a US military surgeon carried out an examination 'with a beer in one hand and making obscene jokes', Fujiwara requested that they stop letting American soldiers other than surgeons witness the examinations (Hirai 2007: 103). With reference to the compulsory VD testing conducted in the territory occupied by German military, Mühlhäuser points out that 'These examinations were probably a very unpleasant procedure for many women. Medical staff would palpate the woman's genitals externally and internally to identify any potential swelling or changes to the skin texture, and the doctors usually not only took blood samples but also performed smear tests and asked the women about their sexual history' (Mühlhäuser 2020: 154).

Thus, from the hospital's viewpoint, the history of compulsory VD examinations may be regarded as a negative legacy, and this may be the reason why they took steps to delete the records. However, for the women who were forced to undergo screenings and treatment with or without their consent, this erasure is unacceptable.

The lawsuit initiated by the Korean women of the US base towns will thus encourage Japanese women who have been through similar experiences and will also provide global audiences with an effective reminder that this kind of testing is a form of sexual violence perpetrated against women in occupied territories.

'Comfort' facilities, relationships and the children of mixed ethnic heritage: a comparative approach

In this book, three main research areas were discovered through comparisons between the German occupied territories during World War II and Japan under the Occupation: first, the recreation (or 'comfort') facilities for the occupying forces; second, the contact between occupying soldiers and women of the occupied territories; and third, the children born of those interactions.

Firstly, regarding the comfort facilities of the occupying forces, in the case of Japan there was only one kind for GHQ, whereas for the German Army, there were two kinds of sex work facilities, one for the Wehrmacht and the other within concentration camps.

Women who were forced into sex work within concentration camps suffered from discrimination as prostitutes not only in the facilities but even after the camps were dismantled (Himeoka 2018). Specifically, at the concentration camps, 'other women inmates were prejudiced against those who were regarded as prostitutes and thought it natural that they were placed at the bottom of the camp hierarchy' (Himeoka 2018: 239). Himeoka also reveals that even in the families that held positive acceptance for the memories of family members who were victims of the Nazis, suppression of the stories was common once there was awareness that sexual violence had occurred. For example, a woman who told her husband about her experiences at the camp had to endure his reproach for the rest of his life, and even after his death, she remained single and never spoke about the matter again. Another woman was too ashamed to tell her story to her mother or to her children (Himeoka 2018: 244). In other words, women who were forced to work as prostitutes inside concentration camps were subjected to extensive discrimination. The way the prostitution facilities recruited workers is similar to the way it occurred in occupied Japan: first of all, the women sent to the camps for sex work were the first to engage in forced sex labor. In both situations 'prostitutes' were treated as 'commodities'.

Secondly, regarding women who had intimate relations with German soldiers in German-occupied France, Roberts reveals that there were two types of women who were subjected to stigma. One was women who had their heads shaved as punishment following the German retreat because they were former lovers of German soldiers. The other was women who were called *boniche* when they became intimate with US soldiers, liberation army soldiers (Roberts 2015: 169). The fact that *boniche* emerged under special postwar circumstances and were often the children of 'good families' who chose to associate with US soldiers as lovers or 'fiancées' reflects the situation of the Japanese women who were called *panpan*. Roberts made a similar comparison between *panpan* and *boniche* (Roberts 2015: 169).

Akiko Fujimori (2016) elucidates the later situations of women who had their heads shaved. Similar stories can also be found in the autobiographies of Kruger (2007) and Lardreau (2010). In 2005, the ANEG was established in France for children born to German soldiers and French women, which also concerns the following point.

Thirdly, regarding children born to Occupation soldiers and women of occupied territories, the comparative scope of this book has made it possible to study the differences in the derogatory terms with which they were labelled. Children born to German soldiers and women of the occupied territories, for example, were called Boche (a derogatory term for Germans) babies, whereas those born of US soldiers and Japanese women were called *panpan* babies. In contrast to the French case, it is interesting that these children were never called Yankee babies or something similar. As discussed in Chapter 8, the expression '*panpan* babies' refers to the mother's position rather than the father's. Mothers are not only 'women who have gone over to the side of the victors' but are also thus discriminated against by society and stigmatized in multiple ways including being viewed as 'prostitutes for the occupying soldiers', 'women who lost her virginity before marriage', and 'women who were deserted by the victor's soldiers'. Since their relationships with the victors did not result in marriage, society never took issue with the responsibilities of the fathers. Here we see the stern gaze of the Japanese patriarchal system towards 'women who lost their virginity before marriage'. Children born of these relations are therefore regarded as *panpan* babies. In the case of the Boche babies, their fathers were soldiers who were driven out of France after turning from the victorious into the defeated. Because of this difference, I reiterate that it is even more difficult for the *panpan* babies to talk about their experiences than it is for the Boche babies.

Inspired by the Boche babies' ability to speak out positively about their own previously concealed experiences, this book has identified what is needed for the Japanese women who were in relationships with but did not formally marry occupying soldiers to be able to talk about their own romances publicly. For the Boche babies, the emergence of 'caring and empathetic listeners' was vital for the telling of their stories. For the Japanese women to start talking about their relationships with occupying soldiers, they too need such listeners. To listen to them carefully and empathetically, we must question our own position of having allowed their stigmatization as *panpan* to go on for such a long time.

A narrative of hope

In addition to the importance of 'caring and empathetic listeners', let me cite three examples that show the possibility of women starting to recount their relationships with the Occupation soldiers that did not lead to marriage. The first is the narrative of Nanoka, who appeared earlier in this book; the second is a story told by Teruyo, who supported women in relationships with soldiers; and the last features the friendly exchanges between the 'women of the night' and singer Shizuko Kasagi and the viewpoints of the journalists who reported these stories.

The hospital director where Nanoka was admitted, who supported her romance with the occupying soldier

The Ueno method (Chizuko Ueno's method of qualitative analysis) advocates being 'betrayed in a pleasant way through an unexpected discovery outside one's narrow view' (Ueno, Ichinomiya and Chazono, eds., 2017: 6). A good example of this is found in the case discussed in Chapter 4 that features Nanoka. While Nanoka was hospitalized for an extended period because of a VD, her soldier boyfriend returned to his home country. This in itself is a common story. Before studying this case, I had a hypothesis: women of occupied nations may have the capacity to control the situation if they are from a high social strata. This hypothesis was made at the point where I was preparing a matrix, at a late stage in my analysis of sixty-three informants who participated in the *Streetwalkers* survey.[3] Matrixes here are two-dimensional planes, such as Table 4.1 (see page 78) and Table 5.1 (see page 106). Let's look at Table 4.1 again, as it includes Nanoka.

Based on this table, I formulated the hypothesis as follows: given the overwhelmingly asymmetrical power relationship between the occupier and the occupied, the more resources the Japanese occupied women have, such as education, wealth, connections and good looks, the better positioned they are in their dealings with occupying soldiers.

Re-examining Nanoka's narrative carefully, however, it was clear that the above hypothesis did not apply to her case. As explained in Chapter 4, since Nanoka left formal education after the fourth year of elementary school, her writing was mostly in *hiragana* and generally quite poor. Her family belonged to a low social stratum. In other words, she was a woman with few resources in education, wealth, connections or good looks. She was working in a cinema where she met an Occupation soldier and fell in love with him. Soon after this, she was admitted to Heian Hospital with a VD. Her soldier boyfriend visited her in the hospital every day. He gave her five yen every two months, and while she was in hospital, 'he brought chocs, cigs, butter, bread and food'. This relationship continued until the soldier returned home. Venereal disease hospitals in this period were managed tightly to prevent inpatients from running away (Chazono 2014). However, in Nanoka's case, on the day her soldier boyfriend was due to be repatriated, the hospital's director allowed her to see him off at the nearest station. Of the sixty-three women in this study, Nanoka was possibly in the furthest position from power, and yet through interactions with two people in different positions of power – that is, the occupying soldier and the hospital director – she managed to take an active role in controlling her situation. The real appeal of the Ueno method lies in the 'pleasant betrayal' of the hypothesis, and at the end of the matrix analysis, I was indeed pleasantly surprised by Nanoka's survival strategy. This unexpected result brings hope for the women who did not marry their soldier boyfriends to start talking about their experiences.

Teruyo, who supported women with occupying soldier boyfriends

The second narrative of hope concerns the acts of Teruyo, as narrated by her daughter Kazu. In spite of living through the Occupation era, Kazu says that she 'never saw' any arrests by MPs of women like homeless dogs. During the Occupation, her mother established a ramen noodle restaurant in Sakyo ward, Kyoto. Although it started as a humble street stall, the shop is now very well-known. After the business began to take off, it attracted all sorts of customers including occupying soldiers, their girlfriends, tax officers and policemen. Even the late singer/actress Hibari Misora dropped by as a girl – a visit which Kazu, who was about the same age as the star, still remembers well.

Kazu recounted an interesting episode about Teruyo, who often offered free bowls of ramen as bribes to the policemen who came in VD arrest vans. Possibly thanks to the bribery, when the testing vans stopped in front of Teruyo's restaurant, 'big sisters' turned up from all over the place and voluntarily got into the van, waving to Kazu 'I'll be home soon!' It may be the effect of Teruyo's ramen bribes that Kazu never encountered a scene akin to a dog-catcher roundup. Teruyo, who had worked as a nurse in Fukuoka when she was single, also assisted at abortions for women in relationships with soldiers, without telling their parents. She was also a journalist for a newspaper publishing company, Kyoto Nichinichi Shimbunsha (today's Kyoto Shimbunsha),[4] and acted as the women's confidante. At this time, Teruyo's restaurant was a contact zone and she played the role of 'intermediary' between the women and the soldiers.

What is notable in these two cases (Nanoka's and Teruyo's) is that people like the VD hospital director and Teruyo actively assisted Japanese women in their sexual liaisons with occupying soldiers. These women survived the Occupation era sometimes by using the power of the soldiers and occasionally by acting in ways that the soldiers did not expect. By focusing on these women's actions, it has emerged that there were supporters around them. Nishikawa finds similarity between these supporters and people she herself encountered as she moved from one community to another, and from one workplace to another, who offered assistance when she faced difficulties as a newcomer. She writes:

> Those who were the first to talk to people in need probably felt that they themselves were outsiders for one reason or another in their respective communities. There were more people in Kyoto during the Occupation than at any other time who were unable to define their place in the city or to find an affiliation to belong to. (Nishikawa 2017: 76–77)

Teruyo was born in Hiroshima. After her stint working as a nurse in Fukuoka, she went to Kyoto, where she worked as a taxi driver and then a journalist. During this time, she got married and had Kazu, continuing her work. After the defeat, she started the ramen stall, but she was unable to open it on rainy days. Then a neighbor offered to rent an empty house for her to use as a restaurant. It might be the case that she helped the women dating the soldiers because she probably thought of herself as a kind of 'outsider' as well. The hospital director who assisted Nanoka, too, may also have been an individual who felt like a stranger.

There must have been many others who supported the women who were called *panpan*.[5] However, to date society has paid too little attention to people like Teruyo. I believe that awareness about this is an important element to enable the women called *panpan* to start talking about their experiences.

The 'women of the night' love the queen of the boogie-woogie, Shizuko Kasagi

Singer Shizuko Kasagi was loved by the so-called 'women of the night', who were of course more commonly known as *panpan*. An article titled 'Go, Shii-chan! Flowers for Kasagi: The queen of the boogie-woogie and the women of the night', published in the *Yomiuri shimbun* on 30 May 1949, reports that Kasagi received a bouquet of flowers from these women at the finale of her show at the Nichigeki (Nihon Gekijo) theater. The article included a photograph of the smiling Kasagi in costume with the leader of the group, O-Yone of Rakucho (i.e. Yurakucho), who presented the flowers to the singer. What motivated O-Yone and her friends to gift flowers to Kasagi stemmed from an incident ten days earlier.

After hearing that Kasagi was performing at Nichigeki after a long absence, around seventy 'women of the night' from

Yurakucho, Yokohama and Omiya gathered at the theater in support of the singer, only to find that the performance had been cancelled because the previous evening the star had fallen from the stage into the orchestra pit during a particularly passionate song rendition. The following day, twenty-eight of the group visited the theater again, this time shocked to find that all the flowers displayed in the foyer were for Kasagi's co-star, Katsuhiko Haida. At the end of the show, too, Haida had received many bouquets from women, but no one had offered any flowers to Kasagi. This prompted O-Yone to organize flowers for her from the group.

As an example of Kasagi's warm and sympathetic personality, the newspaper article cites an episode about her taking home a vagrant child from Kyushu, which impressed the popular comedian Enoken (Ken'ichi Enomoto) so much that he decided to adopt the child. It is notable that Kasagi's support from women like O-Yone was not one-sided; rather, there was a mutually supportive scaffolding established between them.[6] In this case this meant that the warm-hearted Kasagi sang with all her heart for O-Yone and her friends, who, in return, frequented her concerts. In her Osaka dialect, Kasagi describes how 'Every day a group of twenty or thirty of them come to my show. Knowing what sort of hardships they had to go through to save that money brings me to tears'. As Kasagi notes, O-Yone and the others used part of their living allowances in order to buy tickets to her shows. The article goes on to explain that 'Kasagi's circumstances as a single mother making a living by herself have attracted their deep sympathy – so much so that they are eager to support her so that she will become Japan's top singer'. Clearly O-Yone and the other women fully appreciated how hard it was for Kasagi to live in occupied Japan as a single mother.

About a year after this article, the *Mainichi shimbun* (13 June 1950) published an article titled 'Farewell! Women of the night seeing off Shizuko Kasagi', reporting about a special send-off recital at Nichigeki before the singer's tour to the US via Hawaii (which was not yet a US state). Out of more than 3,000 fans, the article describes:

> [A]bout three hundred Night Angels from places including Yurakucho, Ueno, Shinjuku, Ikebukuro, who admire Kasagi as their "big sister" and have cultivated a beautiful friendship with her, were positioned in the prime front row seats that they had reserved early. [Throughout the performance,] they let out waves of shrill, encouraging cheers, before presenting their heart-felt gift of flowers.

The newspaper shows a photograph of Kasagi standing on stage with a huge bouquet that almost covers her face and a number of women standing around her waiting to shake hands with her. The photograph's caption reads 'Women of the night give flowers to Kasagi Shizuko', and there is not a single man in sight around the star.

While media reports on 'women of the night' and *panpan* tend to adopt negative viewpoints, these two articles assume a favorable tone towards those gathered around Kasagi. The first article in the *Yomiuri shimbun* remarks, 'As she [Kasagi] holds a sympathetic stance towards these women of the night, who are often looked down upon by society, they, too, love and admire her. Their friendship adds a pleasant aspect to the early summer show'. In the second *Mainichi* article, it is interesting that the word *panpan* is avoided in favor of 'night angel'. These sympathetic reports were made possible because of the presence of Kasagi as 'intermediary'. Kasagi's show played the role of a contact zone between the group and the journalists who reported on the women's relationship with her. The existence of an 'intermediary' like Kasagi, who also acts as a mutual supporter, was vital for the women called *panpan* to redefine their experiences.

'Something like the outline of a void': the remaining questions

The concluding chapter of Nishikawa's *Koto no Senryo* (The old capital under occupation) begins with this comment:

> Looking back at the whole project, I wonder what I have managed to discover about Kyoto during the Occupation. Many things are still unclear. Perhaps all I have discovered is that I now know what I don't know. The blank parts of the archive, something like an outline of a void, are starting to emerge at last. We must not read this blankness superficially. Now that we know of the existence of the void, however, we must endeavor to trace its outline. (Nishikawa 2017: 323)

The title of this section adopts Nishikawa's expression: 'something like the outline of a void'. This is because I, too, have discovered some 'blank spots in the archive' in my examination of the relationships between occupied women and occupying soldiers, with special attention paid to rape, sex work, love and marriage. Below I explain five main points.

1 The diversity and complexity of women in occupied Japan

There is a folk duo called Kami Fusen (Paper Balloon), composed of a married couple, Yasuyo Hirayama and Etsujiro Goto, who sing a song called 'Takeda Lullaby'. Prior to forming their duo, they were part of a group called Akai Tori (Red

Bird) which disbanded in 1974. In an *Asahi shimbun* article titled 'Beyond discrimination (1): Our "Takeda Lullaby"' (19 January 2010), Hirayama and Goto talk about why they continue to sing the song.

> This song has become immersed in our bodies. So we believe it will reach the audience and become immersed in their bodies too. (Hirayama)
> "Takeda Lullaby" is the utterance of each and every childminder. It's one of the origins of folksongs as well as our starting point. (Goto)

Goto refers to a quotation by a female resident of a Kyoto *buraku* (lit. village, used to signify specific areas subjected to centuries of systematic discrimination) who described 'Takeda Lullaby' 'as a working song about the childminders' hardships and grievances as well as their own self-comfort'.

According to Miki Yamane (1983–2012), who was an activist-scholar deeply concerned about gender and racism, young women from *buraku* were subjected to 'deep-rooted discrimination' (Yamane 2017: 14). Specifically, instead of being employed in textile factories where working conditions were appalling but at least included wages and dormitories, these girls were sent to work as live-in childminders in order to help their own families financially by relieving their living costs. Aged from about five to ten, the childminders would gather together and sing the lullaby as a kind of 'labor song' through which they could express their 'annoyance about the babies who would not stop crying, as well as complaints about their employers and other grievances' (Yamane 2017: 14).

At first, Goto of Kami Fusen had no idea about where Takeda was or about the history of the song. About thirty years ago, when he and Hirayama invited the woman who sang the original song to a performance, she asked them 'not to sing the song anymore as it brings shame on the *buraku*'. However, the situation has now changed. The duo continue to sing the lullaby, noting, 'The song has become a source of pride for the *buraku* people, and it is sung by chorus groups. We think that's fantastic'. As a result of the duo singing 'Takeda Lullaby' for thirty years, women from the discriminated *buraku* have been able to redefine their experiences.

Amongst the sixty-three women whose stories were examined in this book, there may be some who in their own girlhoods were childminders who sang 'Takeda Lullaby'. If this is the case, their association with the occupying soldiers may signify 'liberation' from 'deep-rooted discrimination'. However, judging from their narratives, whether there were in fact any such women among the sixty-three remains a 'blank'.

Another example of blankness in the *panpan* data concerns Korean residents of Japan who are referred to as *zainichi* Koreans. Nishikawa poses the important question as to whether 'the category of "those who did not possess Japanese citizenship during the Occupation period" includes people who were originally from former Japanese colonies and had lived in Kyoto for many years, such as *zainichi* Koreans and other nationalities'. This question arose from the fact that 'schools in Kansai had one or two children repatriated (*hikiage jido*) from the Korean peninsula in each class and about the same or larger numbers of *zainichi* Korean children' (Nishikawa 2017: 280). The data on the sixty-three women is blank on this topic as well.

If some of the women associated with the occupying soldiers had 'blank' (undocumented) experiences, and if 'the void should not be read superficially', examples – such as Kami

Fusen, who continue to sing 'Takeda Lullaby', Yamane, who identified a 'small protest packed with anger and grievances' in girls from the *buraku* 'against a historical background weighing heavily on them' (Yamane 2017: 14), and Nishikawa, who drew attention to the presence of *zainichi* Korean children at schools in Kansai during the Occupation period – suggest that it is possible that 'blank' experiences may cease to become so. Since more than seventy years have passed since the end of the war, the blank spots may never be filled in these women's lifetimes. However, even an awareness of such experiences of 'blankness' will enable us to share the perspectives of Kami Fusen, Yamane and Nishikawa. This will lead to our discovery of the survival strategies of the women who endured the contact zones.

2 The racial diversity and complexity of the occupying soldiers

Nishikawa points out that 'During the Occupation, military bases and other places containing military secrets were whited out in maps of Japan' (2017: 323). While this is a reference to the invisible 'blank' spaces on the maps of Kyoto under Occupation, such areas were not limited to that city. As repeatedly discussed in this book, the Occupation of Japan was a period when GHQ's freedom of speech controls censored newspapers, magazines and documents. Directly relevant to this book is the censorship of the narratives of the sixty-three women reported in *Streetwalkers* by GHQ, which redacted the sections concerning the occupying soldiers who were partners or clients of these women. This means that information about the ethnic backgrounds of the soldiers is also absent.

Besides black and white soldiers, the Occupation forces also included Japanese-Americans. The CIC (Counter Intelligence Corps) during the Japanese Occupation, especially, consisted of second generation Japanese-Americans (Nikkei nisei). According to historian Eiji Takemae, they fully utilized their language skills and similarities in skin color and facial appearance to thoroughly collect information in all fields (Takemae 1983: 106). In light of this background, the following point Nishikawa makes is important:

> During the Occupation, intelligence activities continued behind the backs of residents. In the process of gathering intelligence, officers had to contact residents. There must have been residents and informants who actively or unknowingly offered information. (Nishikawa 2017: 349)

Therefore, some Japanese women may have had intimate relationships with second generation Japanese-American soldiers who were neither white nor black but looked like Japanese nationals. In fact, many women may have felt closer to Nikkei soldiers who looked similar to them, and their parents may have given approval more easily if their daughters' boyfriends had have been Nikkei rather than white or black soldiers. However, those Nikkei soldiers may have approached the Japanese women and established romantic relationships with them with the intention of collecting information. According to Yasutomi's research, 8,381 Japanese women married occupying soldiers, including civilians in military employment. Of these men, seventy-two percent were white, fifteen percent second generation Japanese-Americans, and twelve percent black (Yasutomi 2005b: 208–209). The fact that more women married Nikkei soldiers than black soldiers likely means that the number of relationships that did not lead to marriage was also larger, along with the number of children born of those relationships.[7]

Considering all this information, let us return to the question of why the 'yellow' (Asian) mixed children were excluded from the Ministry of Welfare's investigation, as discussed in Chapter 8. As we saw, Kano conjectures that it may be because 'yellow' mixed heritage children were regarded as more likely to be integrated into the 'Japanese' category. Besides this theory, there is also the possibility that the fathers of the 'yellow' mixed children may have been staff of the CIC, and were accordingly removed from the investigation. Information about the 'yellow' mixed children remains blank. As the historian Taihei Okada points out, in occupied Japan, 'it is important to compare and contrast the racial categories among Japanese and various racial/ethnic identities of other peoples' (2017: 87). This is pertinent to research on women in relationships with occupying soldiers: depending on the race and ethnicity of the soldiers, the Japanese around these women must have looked at them in different ways, which in turn must have affected the women's experiences in more ways than this book has revealed.

3 The 'void' of racial information on occupying soldiers in relationships with German women

The 7 May 1952 *Mainichi shimbun* issue includes an article titled 'Severe discrimination – abandoned black-skinned children: The issue of 4,000 mixed-race German children'. It reports that children born of the Allied Forces' white soldiers and German women are 'not so much of an issue' as their parents are Caucasians. In contrast, mixed-race children born of German women and Soviet soldiers in East Germany, black units of the US Army, and 'Moroccans and others brought in by the French Army' are reported to 'have caused considerable issues'. According to an unofficial estimate, it continues, there are 4,000 'mixed-race (black and white) children' in West Germany with black American or Moroccan fathers and white German mothers. Most of these children had been secretly sent by their reputation-fearing mothers to orphanages and childcare centers and raised there. However, as the article notes, seven years had then passed since the end of the war, and these children were reaching school age, which had considerably 'complicated the problem'. In particular, it points out the intense discrimination against black people in Germany, and how around the time when the first group of children of the Allied Forces were starting school, similar concerns were also emerging in Japan.

The same article touches upon the topic of racism in Germany, stating that while ostensibly there is no discriminatory treatment, in reality colored people are regarded as inferior among the general population. Specific examples include cases especially in the small cities and rural areas of Southern Germany where mixed-race children are subject to discrimination from other children and laborers and are often blatantly refused entry to childcare and family care facilities. It also recounts a case where a photograph published in a magazine featured a child praying every day for their skin to turn white. Only ten percent of black fathers and white mothers were married, and ninety percent of the fathers had already returned to the US. When mothers made petitions to the US authorities, they adopted a non-interference policy, regarding parental responsibilities as personal matters between ordinary men and women. The article concludes with the controversial matter of whether white children's schools will accept children with colored fathers.

While the article shows that there was a clear difference (even more blatant than in Japan) between mixed-background children with white fathers and those with black fathers, when it came to children with Asian fathers,[8] a 'void' prevails.

Even if counter-intelligence acts were carried out in Germany as in Japan, it is hard to imagine that Nikkei soldiers would have been used for such activities in Germany, suggesting that the lack of coverage on Asian-mixed children must be due to issues on the part of the Japanese.

It is therefore necessary to carry out comparative studies of occupied Europe and Asia, including the issue of mixed-marriage children with Asian heritages.

4 French women: 'boniche' women and their children

In this book, I have repeatedly discussed the women in France labelled '*boniche*', who had associations with soldiers of the liberation forces. However, there are some issues that I could not examine sufficiently in the present study. For instance, what happened to these women in their later lives and what kinds of experiences did their children have? How did other French people see these women? Were *boniche* children as stigmatized as *panpan* babies? Further comparative investigations into the experiences of the *boniche* and *panpan* women and their children are called for. At the same time, it is necessary to investigate whether children of German fathers are all regarded as Boche babies regardless of the ethnicity of their mothers.[9]

While acknowledging the importance of 'being conscious that voices of those directly involved are somehow lost in the process' (Narita 2018: 280), we must aim at conducting collaborative studies and exchanging opinions with researchers

Photo 9.1 American women in a convertible

Photo 9.2 American women on a boat deck

of the inter-war and occupation periods in various parts of Asia and Europe.

5 The impact of female military and paramilitary personnel upon women of the occupied territories

Finally, regarding female military and paramilitary personnel posted in occupied Japan, the present study dealt with only one example, that of Virginia Olson, who went to Japan as a

Photo 9.3 American women walking through the streets of occupied Japan

Photo 9.4 American women at Asakusa liberty market

nurse. Here let us look at four photographs, focusing on the fashion of the American women in them. The original images are color photographs.

The convertible in Photo 9.1 is blue, and each of the women in it is wearing colorful clothes. The woman standing up in the driver's seat wears a red jacket and a light blue coat, and the others are dressed in bright colors as well. In Photo 9.2, featuring a number of women on a boat deck, the woman in the center is wearing an eye-catching red beret. The woman on the right in Photo 9.3 is wearing a white dress with red embroidery, a head scarf wrapped around her head with the same pattern, and red sandals. The woman on the left is wearing a white dress with a black belt, carrying a black jacket over her left arm. In Photo 9.4, the woman on the far left wears a brown suit (possibly a uniform), while the one in the middle is in a green suit, and the one on the right wears a red coat, a pale blue skirt and a blue scarf wrapped around her head. Everyone is dressed in bright colors. On the right side of the image a group of Japanese women in kimonos are huddled together, looking at the three foreign women. It is striking that while the three foreign women stand there smiling, the Japanese women stare at them with stern expressions.

What is common to each of these photographs is that at least one woman is wearing a head scarf. I have seen photographs of *panpan* with scarves wrapped around their heads before, but looking at these four images again, I wonder if the fashion of the *panpan* was influenced by that of American women. Scarves are handy and economical fashion items that can be made easily from a piece of cloth and used in various ways. Using scraps of kimono, they could even create something that would not be found in America.

Quite a number of the sixty-three informants mentioned that they were learning dressmaking, and many were interested in fashion, as in the case of Natsuko (aged twenty), who said that she read magazines such as *Style* and *Beauty* (mentioned in Chapter 4). They saw American women like the ones in the above photographs in their everyday lives. It is also easy to imagine that some Japanese women may have been influenced by the behavior of these American women. In particular, the sight of women driving around unchaperoned in a convertible (as in Photo 9.1) must have aroused curiosity among some Japanese women, especially those who were interested in having relationships with the occupying soldiers.

Thus, given that the lifestyle of American women in the occupied territories may have influenced the Japanese women in intimate relationships with Occupation soldiers, it is clear that female soldiers and civilians working for the Allied Forces need further consideration.

The agency of the women surviving the contact zones and their survival strategies

Women in intimate relationships with Occupation soldiers were overwhelmingly in a weaker position in the power structure of the time. How did they negotiate, then, with the soldiers who held the power? What sort of survival strategies and agency (independent actions) did they use to survive the Occupation? Contact zones of mutual negotiation between the Occupation soldiers and the women of the occupied territories are neither limited to Japan nor to the past. Women of the Occupation era overlap with local women of various regions who are engaged in mutual negotiations with the soldiers stationed in those regions. They share some similar experiences with Korean women, for example, in camp towns around US military bases, fighting for survival, negotiating daily with American soldiers, and using their strategies and agency.

One important point about agency is that one salient socially accepted narrative of victims of sexual violence involves the women being 'model victims', deprived of agency. Ueno notes:

> If agency marks the border between the narratable and the unnarratable stories of sexual violence, the victim's agency ought to be denied. Even though their experiences are on a continuum, agency divides them. (Ueno 2018: 11)

As we saw in the examples discussed in this book, common to all the women who relayed their experiences of being raped by Occupation soldiers is the fact that they fit the 'model victim' category of a sexually innocent woman who fiercely resisted being attacked by an unknown soldier. Because of this position, they could talk about their experiences of being rape victims to the investigators. Sato makes an important point in relation to this:

> In order to understand the complex and diverse states of sexual violence surrounding war, it is necessary to consider both women's agency and the structural violence of gender relations, both of which can manifest under any circumstances. Such considerations are vital for the fight to eliminate sexual violence in wartime and in peacetime. (2018: 337)

Even when women do show their agency, the violence against them should never be overlooked, nor should their voices be silenced. This is because with the overwhelmingly asymmetrical power relationship of the ruling and the ruled, agency is used by the oppressed women to survive difficult situations. This very use of agency is their survival strategy.

Under various circumstances, a wide range of women in occupied territories have had relationships with occupying soldiers. Their experiences have been forced into silence, along with the stigma of the *panpan*. We should not allow this erasure to perpetuate. We must acknowledge and respect their diverse survival strategies, reminding ourselves that we might have done the same had we been in their situations. Through this acknowledgement, we can become their 'caring and empathetic listeners'. Only then can they begin to start talking about their experiences, which, in turn, will lead to the restoration of their honor, including that of those who are deceased and are unable to tell their own stories. The agency of the women survivors of the contact zones emerged out of the individual case studies included in this book. In this agency, it is my sincere wish to discover the survival strategies of the vulnerable and to restore their voices to history. I cannot overemphasize this point.[10]

Notes

Introduction

1. The interview was conducted as part of a documentary program on the anniversary of the end of the war, 'Sengo zeronen' (0 years after the war) broadcast on 15 August 2015 on NHK-BS.

2. Photos in this chapter are titled according to American soldier personal photograph captions. All photos were of Kobe City immediately following the Occupation. All photographs are the property of Taichi Kinugawa.

3. Written on the photograph are the words: 'CPL. PERSE LOOKING OVER SOME NEW GEISHA GIRLS'.

4. The Weekly Summary of Events gave a week-by-week account of the number and details of incidents involving military personnel. See RG331/SCAP/Box 9894 (c).

Chapter 1

1. Cultural anthropologist Masakazu Tanaka expands on Pratt's concept of contact zones as 'areas where contact occurs between people of different cultural backgrounds' (2011a: 11). His work positions Japanese society during the Occupation as a contact zone, and analyzes discourses concerning *panpan* from various perspectives, including those of Japanese intellectuals, activists and children (2011b). For further information, refer to the work of Okada (2017), which collates previous research on *panpan* during the Occupation period from various fields of study (women's studies, literary studies etc.). For a detailed analysis of discourses from the perspectives of the Occupation forces, see Kasama (2012) and Aoki (2013).

2. The Hyogo Prefectural Police Department provides representative examples of the realities of the establishment of comfort facilities for the Occupation forces. The details of these descriptions, along with those of Kanagawa prefecture to the east and Hiroshima prefecture to the west, are considered to be the three most important accounts of the era, as introduced by Yoshiaki Yoshimi and Myoung-suk Yun (1996: 60–63).

3. For an example of the 'offering' of unmarried women from pioneer settlements to Soviet army officers in exchange for the protection of settlements and food security, see Inomata (2018).

4. The SS was not a national army, but a Nazi (National Socialist German Workers' Party) organisation. After seizing power, it merged with the police, and played three central roles in the Holocaust: the management of concentration camps and killings in the death camps; the rounding up of Jews and locking them in or transferring them to ghettoes; and mass shootings. The SS Reich Leader and German Police Commissioner was Heinrich Himmler. For more information on the relationship between the Wehrmacht and the SS, see Mühlhäuser (2015: xxxv; please note that this section does not appear in the English version published in 2020).

5. To date, not much is known about the actual circumstances that led women to work in the prostitution facilities set up for the Wehrmacht, but Mühlhäuser suggests that it is likely that many women applied for the work voluntarily. Additionally, however, Mühlhäuser points out that the boundary between voluntary and forced recruitment is quite fluid in such cases (2020: 155).

6. American soldier personal photograph caption. Photo was of Kobe City immediately following the Occupation. Photo is the property of Taichi Kinugawa.

7. For more information on these recruitment advertisements in Kobe at the time, see Chazono (2014); for nationwide advertisements, see Hirai (2014).

8. The Recreation and Amusement Association (RAA; lit., Special Comfort Facility Association) took advantage of the chaos in the wake of the war with an attractive recruitment advertisement: 'Urgent notice: Special female employees wanted. Food, clothing, accommodation and luxury items provided in advance. Travel expenses paid to applicants from the provinces' (*Yomiuri shimbun*, 3 September 1945). The 'special female employees' were of course sexual comfort women for Occupation soldiers. There are detailed accounts of the establishment of the RAA in Sugiyama (1988) and Hirai (2014).

9. The Oita Prefectural Council also had a problem with innocent women being falsely arrested and treated as prostitutes (Chazono 2014: 196).

10. See 'GHQ Materials' section of the Bibliography for details on this source.

11. See St Luke's International Hospital 'History' webpage: http://hospital.luke.ac.jp/eng/about/history/index.html

12. The Ryo Suzuki Seminar (College of Social Sciences, Ritsumeikan University), *Senryoka no Kyoto* (Kyoto Under Occupation) (Bunrikaku, 1991), is a joint research project by students on the theme of 'Social Historical Analysis of Postwar Japan: Kyoto in the Period of Postwar Reform'. It is an extremely important resource in elucidating details on Kyoto during the Occupation.

13. This figure is based on the results of a survey of local civil servant salaries conducted on 1 April 2015, by the Survey Section of the Salary Efficiency Promotion Office in the Public Services Department of the Local Administration Bureau, under the Ministry of Internal Affairs and Communications. See http://www.soumu.go.jp/main_sosiki/jichi_gyousei/c-gyousei/kyuuyo/pdf/h27_kyuyo_1_03.pdf (viewed 26 March 2017).

Chapter 2

1. The two men were a corporal and a common solider in the 1st Cavalry Division. This incident was reported in GHQ CID's Weekly Summary of Events of 7 July 1950. The rapes by Occupation soldiers discussed in this book are all taken from RG331/SCAP/Box 9894 (c).

2. Weekly Summary of Events, 9 June 1950.

3. Weekly Summary of Events, 15 June 1950.

4. Weekly Summary of Events, 7 July 1950.

5. '[T]his may be an indication of the pressure many women felt after the end of the war to justify themselves or prove that they had not encouraged the men in any way, but had instead been powerless and helpless', writes Mühlhäuser, arguing that the situation 'might be indicative of a more widespread emphasis on victims having to prove their innocence' (2020: 56).

6. Being a 'dancer' in occupied Japan meant dancing privately with a customer, though not necessarily erotically.

Chapter 3

1. Even though I researched the registry extensively, I could not find precise details about registration. While investigating the public records (collaboratively) from 2015 to 2018 however, I did find a record of the term 'registry' (*jisseki*). Combined with the narratives in *Streetwalkers*, it became clear that during the Occupation period, if women could not produce documents proving their 'registration', they could neither receive rations, work in a company nor rent reasonably priced accommodation. This kind of 'registration' system can thus be seen as a form of proof of personal identification, similar to today's health certificates, passports or driver's licenses. Whether or not a women was registered was the cause for huge economic differences if she fraternized with Occupation soldiers. Most of the women reported in *Streetwalkers* were only 'registered' in their hometowns so, if they left that town they were forced to live off the black market.

2. Dr. Donald V. Wilson, the first assistant manager of GHQ's PHW, Welfare Division, Social Work Training Branch, was a member of the selection committee for local welfare officers in Tochigi prefecture (Akiyama 1978: 241)

Chapter 4

1. When Kazu was a elementary school student, a woman who was kind to her took her to a cabaret in Osaka where she worked as a dancer. According to Kazu, when she finished dancing, she took her tip from the soldier and quickly hid it in Kazu's shoes (interviewed 25 July 2015).

2. I discuss Asa's relationship with her first partner in greater detail in Chapter 5.

3. For example, interviewers substituted the kanji for 'police' (*keisatsu* in Japanese, written *kesatsu* by Nanoka) and hospital-ization (*nyuin* in Japanese, written *iui* by Nanoka).

Chapter 5

1. These results accord with the outcome of interviews conducted by Nishikawa (2017: 239), who found that people who worked in venues where English was used were well educated.

Chapter 6

1. Despite what the investigator wrote in the notes, the lifestyle of Lily – who earned an income as a sex worker and said she 'won't stop working as a *panpan* unless I'm rounded up' – can also perhaps be described as a survival strategy.

Chapter 7

1. Kosaka, who reminisced that 'My love for America started out from such a simple thing, with no particularly deep meaning' (1990: 14), later went on tour performing at Allied Forces' camps around Japan.

2. Rather than identifying specific intermediaries, where various contradictions exist in the relationship between colonizer and colonized, Tanaka (2011b: 164) suggests that a contact zone is characterized by the fact that all entities in this zone become or have the potential to become intermediaries.

3. Sociologist Ikutaro Shimizu, educator Seiichi Miyahara and education critic Shozaburo Ueda collected 1,325 compositions by elementary and middle school students (under the current education system) living near US military bases from Hokkaido in the north to Kagoshima in the south. They then selected 200 compositions for inclusion in their edited book titled *Kichi no ko: Kono jijitsu wo dou kangaetara yoi ka* (Base children: How should we think about this fact?; 1953). The book's 'Report on selection criteria' states that the editors did not choose the included works in line with any 'set ideology'. Other relevant books include *Kichi Nihon* (Base Japan; 1953), edited by Kozo Inomata and Kihachiro Kimura, along with Ikutaro Shimizu, and *Gaisho to kodomotachi: Tokuni kichi Yokosuka-shi no genjo bunseki* (Street prostitutes and children: Focusing on the situation at Yokosuka Base), edited by the Keio University Social Work Research Group, reproduced in *Nihon 'kodomo no*

rekishi' sosho (Japan [children's history] series; 1998). These three books mainly deal with the situation around US bases during the Korean War, a time when the Occupation of Japan had ended but combat-ready soldiers remained stationed there.

4. This means there is a need for research on how the mixed-blood children of women called '*boniches*' were treated.

5. There is a need for intensive research into labels used in Austria, such as 'chocolate girls' and 'Yankee wives'.

Chapter 8

1. Here 'office workers' included, for instance, hospitality worker, lift attendant, hospital assistant and company president's secretary.

2. Kano found that children of 'yellow descent' were excluded from the Ministry of Health and Welfare's survey of 'mixed-blood children' (the document was discovered by historian Kazuko Hirai in Sunto-gun, Shizuoka prefecture). Importantly, she points out that the reason for the exclusion might have been the ministry's assessment that mixed-blood children with 'racially proximate' fathers and 'yellow' skin could be subsumed under the category of Japanese, regardless of whether they were children of the Occupation in terms of their appearance (Kano 2007: 239).

3. Miyoshi Miyazaki, who went to elementary school in Kobe, recalls that there were one or two mixed-blood children in her class. I have been interviewing Ms. Miyazaki, who currently manages a café and event space under the elevated railway in Kobe Motomachi, since 2014. She helped my research by asking people working nearby in the Motomachi shopping arcade about how things were in Kobe under the Occupation.

4. In his comments endorsing *Bosshu no ko* (2007), a Japanese translation of Kruger's book, Shigeru Kashima used 'Doitsu-yaro' (German bastards) as the equivalent for 'Boche', a derogatory term for Germans. In the actual translation of the book, 'Boche' is translated as 'Doitsu-jin' (Germans). I find it rather odd that in her afterword the translator Kimie Ozawa refers to the issue of Japanese war orphans left in China but offers no mention of

children born to Occupation soldiers and Japanese women – nor does she do so in another of her translations, *Hokori takai shojo* (Proud girls, 2010, translated from *Orgueilleuse*). Akiko Fujimori, the author of *Marugari ni sareta onnatachi* (Women who had their head shaved; 2016), does refer to *panpan* in her afterword.

5. The book was later given the new title, *Née d'amours interdites*: *Ma mère était française, mon père, soldat allemand* (Born of forbidden love: My mother was French, my father a German soldier).

6. This is a translation from the Japanese version of Kruger's book.

7. According to Kruger, the documentary was first broadcast in 2002, but the official website for *Enfants de Boches* states that its first television broadcast occurred in 2003.

8. Historical sociologist Shinzo Araragi describes Ishida's practice as 'model stories' to emancipate women victims through a tripartite that involves the victims, listeners and supporters, and he proposes the concept of 'model stories for emancipation'. At the same time, Araragi points out the need to be aware of the risk whereby model stories take on a life of their own and other stories might be suppressed and excluded (2018: 300, 304).

Conclusion

1. It should be noted, however, that the court did not accept the victims' claim that the state illegally established the US base towns to facilitate prostitution. The judgement was based on the view that the victims were neither forced into prostitution in the base towns nor placed in a situation in which they could not avoid prostitution.

2. Although hardly known in Japan, it is important to note that members of the PHW (Public Health and Welfare Section) lodged a formal complaint about the MP treating Japanese women as criminals when they were found to be suffering from VDs in the compulsory examinations. The PHW emphasized that 'Cases of venereal disease must be accepted and treated courteously as "patients" and not as "criminals"' (Thomas 1947 RG331/E1851/9370 part 2; Chazono 2014: 202).

3. The Ueno method is a further development of the conventional KJ method in that it combines case analysis with code analysis when analyzing data, in the contexts of both the case and its comparisons (Ueno 2017b: 37). In regard to Table 4.1 of this book, the vertical axis shows the case analysis (of Kanon, Ran, Karin, Yukiko and other women) which is combined with the code analysis of the horizontal axis (comparative analysis of age, education, finance, connection, appearance, previous work, current address). Analyses based on the conventional KJ method would not be as thorough as this.

4. At the time of the Occupation, there were two companies that were called Kyoto Nichinichi Shimbunsha. Teruyo worked in the one that was to become Kyoto Shimbunsha, according to the informant, the late Noriko Kitahara.

5. Cosmetic surgeon Katsuya Takasu's grandmother, for example, acted as a consultant for women who fraternized with soldiers during the Occupation, and offered free surgical treatment. She, too, supported the *panpan* women (Saibara 2016: chap. 'LOVE 040', n.p.).

6. Mutual support providers include people who offered rented rooms to women who had relations with Occupation soldiers. For example, the film director Seijun Suzuki who made a film version of Taijiro Tamura's novel *Nikutai no mon* (Gate of flesh) depicting the everyday life of women working as *panpan* recalls that in 1949 his wages were so low that to make ends meet, he let two such women use his room to receive soldiers in exchange for money (Yomota, ed., 2010: 90). The relationship between Suzuki and the women was one of mutual support.

7. Hayashi interviewed a woman who married a Nikkei nisei and went to the US. She met her husband while he was posted in Tokyo as a US Navy intelligence officer (Hayashi 2002: 29). It is not clear whether the intelligence service organization was the CIC.

8. In Yukiko Kimura's collection of interviews with war brides in Hawaii, archived at the University of Hawaii at Manoa's RASRL (Romanzo Adams Social Research Laboratory), there are

interviews with one German woman married to a soldier with a Chinese background and another German woman married to a Portuguese-Filipino soldier, proving that there are children with mixed-Asian lineage. There are also a number of cases of Japanese women and Okinawan soldiers (from an investigation conducted in November 2015). Scholar of American history Masako Nakamura writes that because German women in prewar and war times under the Nazi regime played gendered roles according to the strict patriarchal system, Nikkei soldiers were attracted to their 'frugal, hardworking and domestic' aspects, which led to some marriages (Nakamura 2007: 155).

9. I plan to re-examine the interviews collected by Yukiko Kimura and others, using the Ueno method, to carry out a comparative study of Asian and European war brides during the Occupation, with their husbands, children and other family relations included in the scope. (This research was started in 2022.)

10. The women of the occupied territories who were in relationships with German soldiers were not necessarily of Aryan descent. Regarding the increased birth rates in enemy countries caused by the 'lack of discipline' on the part of German soldiers, see Mühlhäuser (2020: 245–303).

11. As an associated reference book to the present book, see Chizuko Ueno, Shinzo Araragi and Kazuko Hirai, eds., *Senso to seiboryoku no hikakushi e mukete* (Toward a comparative history of war and sexual violence; 2018). Part II, 'Katari enai kioku' (Memories that cannot be narrated), includes Toshimi Chazono's Chapter 5, 'Sekkusu to iu kontakuto zon: Nihon senryo no keiken kara' (The contact zone called sex: From the experiences of the Occupation of Japan), which summarizes the present study.

Bibliography

Akio, Satoko (2011), *Washinton Haitsu: GHQ ga Tokyo ni kizanda sengo* (Washington Heights: GHQ, engraved in Tokyo after World War II), Shincho Bunko.

Akiyama, Tomohisa (1978), 'Donarudo V Uiruson hakase no "shogen"' (The 'testimony' of Dr. Donald V. Wilson), in Akira Ono (ed.), *Senryoki ni okeru shakaifukushishiryo ni kansuru kenkyuhokokusho* (Report on studies of social welfare documents and data during the Occupation of Japan), Japanese Research Institute on Social Welfare, Inc.

Ando, Nisuke and Yukuo Sasamoto (commentary) (1996), *GHQ Nihon senryo shi 3: Busshi to romu no chotatsu* (History of the nonmilitary activities of the Occupation of Japan, 1945–1951: Logistic support), Yukuo Sasamoto (trans.), Nihon Tosho Center. (The source material was created by GHQ/SCAP, Civil Historical Section.)

Aoki, Shin (2013), *Meguriau monotachi no gunzo: sengo Nihon no beigunkichi to ongaku 1945-1958* (Meetings and crowds: US military bases and music in post-war Japan, 1945–1958), Otsuki Shoten.

Araragi, Shinzo (2018), 'Senjiseiboryokuhigai wo kikitoru to iu koto: "*Odo no mura no seiboryoku*" wo tegakari ni' (To listen to victims of sexual violence in wartime: Using '*Sexual violence in villages in loess regions*'), in Chizuko Ueno, Shinzo Araragi and Kazuko Hirai (eds.), *Senso to seiboryoku no hikakushi e mukete* (Toward a comparative history of war and sexual violence), Iwanami Shoten.

Chazono, Toshimi (2014), *Panpan to wa dare nano ka? Kyacchi to iu senryoki no seiboryoku to GI to no shinmitsusei* (Who were panpan? The catch as a form of sexual violence during the Occupation and intimacy with GIs), Impact Shuppankai.

Chazono, Toshimi (2018), 'Sekkusu to iu kontakuto zon: Nihon senryo no keiken kara' (The contact zone called sex: From the experience of the Occupation of Japan), in Chizuko Ueno, Shinzo Araragi and Kazuko Hirai (eds.), *Senso to seiboryoku no hikakushi e mukete* (Toward a comparative history of war and sexual violence), Iwanami Shoten.

Chazono, Toshimi (2018), *Mouhitotsu no senryo: Sekkusu to iu kontakuto zon kara* (Another Occupation: From the contact zone called sex), Impact Shuppankai.

Fujime, Yuki (1997), *Sei no rekishigaku: koshoseido, dataizaitaisei kara baishunboshiho, yuseihogoho taisei e* (History of sex: From licensed prostitution and criminalized abortion to anti-prostitution laws and legal protections for eugenics), FujiShuppan.

Fujimori, Akiko (2016), *Marugari ni sareta onnatachi: 'Doitsuhei no koibito' no sengo wo tadoru tabi* (Women who had their head shaved: A journey following the post-war experiences of 'German soldiers' lovers'), Iwanami Shoten.

Furukubo, Sakura (1999), 'Manshu ni okeru Nihonjinjosei no keiken: giseishasei no kochiku' (Experiences of Japanese women in Manchuria: Constructing victimhood), *The Annals of Women's History*, 9, Women's History Editorial Committee (ed.).

Goffman, Erving ([1970] 2001), *Sutiguma no shakaigaku: rakuin wo osareta aidentiti*, revised edition, Takeshi Ishiguro (trans.), Serica Shobo. (Translation of *Stigma: Notes on the Management of Spoiled Identity*, published by Penguin in 1963.)

Goto, Chiori (2017), 'Charitigaru: nijuseikishoto no rodo to jenda' (Charity girl: Labor and gender in the early twentieth century), in Kei Hibino and Michiko Shimokobe (eds.), *Amerikan reiba: gasshukoku ni okeru rodo no bunkahyosho* (American labor: Cultural representations of labor in the United States), Sairyusha.

Grossmann, Atina (1995), 'A question of silence: The rape of German women by Occupation soldiers', *October*, vol. 72, Spring, pp. 42–63.

Grossmann, Atina (1999), 'Chinmoku to iu mondai: senryoheishi ni yoru Doitsujyosei no gokan' (A question of silence: The rape of German women by Occupation soldiers), Miho Ogino (trans.), *Shiso (Thought)*, 4, Iwanami Shoten.

Harada, Hiroshi (1994), *MP no jipu kara mita senryoka no Tokyo: dojyokeisatsukan no kansatsuki* (Occupied Tokyo from an MP's jeep: Observations by a passenger police officer), Soshisha.

Harada, Hiroshi (2011), *Aru keisatsukan no Showa sesoshi* (The Showa social history of a police officer), Soshisha.

Hashimoto, Akiko (2015), *The Long Defeat: Cultural Trauma, Memory, and Identity in Japan*, Oxford University Press.

Hashimoto, Akiko (2017), *Nhon no nagai sengo: haisen no kioku, torauma wa dou kataritsugareteiruka* (The long defeat: cultural trauma, memory, and identity in Japan), Yumi Yamaoka (trans.), Misuzu Shobo.

Hayakawa, Noriyo (2007), 'Senryogunheishi no ian to baibaishunsei no saihen' (Revisiting comfort and prostitution systems for occupying soldiers), in Keisen University's Institute for Peace and Culture (ed.), *Senryo to sei: seisaku, jittai, hyosho* (Occupation and sex: Policy, reality and representation), Impact Shuppankai.

Hayashi, Kaori (2002), 'Bei, Go no sensohanayometachi: ikoku de ganbattekita watashitachi wo mite' (War brides in the United States and Australia: How we did our best in a foreign country), in Kaori Hayashi, Keiko Tamura and Fumiko Takatsu, *Sensohanayome: kokkyo wo koeta onnatachi no hanseiki* (War brides: Half a century of women who crossed borders), Fuyo Shobo Publishing.

Hayashi, Kaori (2005), *Watashi wa sensohanayome desu: Amerika to Osutoraria de ikiru Nikkeikokusaikekkonshinbokukai no onnatachi* (I am a war bride: Women from Japanese international marriage community groups in America and Australia), Hokkoku Shimbun Publishing Bureau.

Himeoka, Toshiko (2018), 'Nachi Doitsu no seiboryoku wa ikani fukashika sareta ka: kyoseishuyojyonai baishunshisetsu wo chushin to shite' (How sexual violence in Nazi Germany was made invisible: Focusing on prostitution facilities in concentration camps), in Chizuko Ueno, Shinzo Araragi and Kazuko Hirai (eds.), *Senso to seiboryoku no hikakushi e mukete* (Toward a comparative history of war and sexual violence), Iwanami Shoten.

Hirai, Kazuko (2007), 'RAA and "akasen": Atami ni okeru tenkai' (RAA and 'red lines': The case of Atami), in Keisen University's Institute for Peace and Culture (ed.), *Senryo to sei: seisaku, jittai, hyosho* (Occupation and sex: Policy, reality and representation), Impact Shuppankai.

Hirai, Kazuko (2014), *Nihonsenryo to jyenda: beigun, baibaishun to Nihonjoseitachi* (Gender and the Occupation of Japan: The US military, prostitution and Japanese women), Yushisha.

Hori, Michinori (supv.) and Shizuma Sato (ed.) (1956), *Kobe shiritsu Higashiyama Byoin shi* (History of Higashiyama Hospital, Kobe), Kobe City Health Bureau, Kobe City Higashiyama Hospital.

Hyogo Prefectural Hygiene Department, General Affairs Section (ed.) (1950), *Showa nijuyonendo kokko hojo ni kansuru tsuzuri* (1949 national treasury subsidy booklet), Hyogo Prefectural Hygiene Department, General Affairs Section.

Hyogo Prefectural Police History Compilation Committee (ed.) (1975), *Hyogoken keisatsushi: Showahen* (Hyogo Prefectural Police history: Showa edition), Hyogo Prefectural Police Headquarters.

Inomata, Kozo, Kihachiro Kimura and Ikutaro Shimizu (eds.) (1953), *Kichi Nihon* (Base Japan), Wakosha.

Inomata, Yusuke (2018), 'Kataridashita seiboryoku higaisha: Manshu hikiagesha no giseishagensetsu wo yomitoku' (Victims of sexual violence speaking out: Deciphering the discourse of repatriated victims from Manchuria), in Chizuko Ueno, Shinzo Araragi and Kazuko Hirai (eds.), *Senso to seiboryoku no hikakushi e mukete* (Toward a comparative history of war and sexual violence), Iwanami Shoten.

Ishida, Yoneko (2002), 'Chugoku ni okeru Nihongun seiboryokuhigai no chosa, kiroku ni torikunde: higaijoseitachi no "deguchiki" (kokoro ni wadakamaru mono wo hakidasu) no imi wo kangaeru' (Investigating and recording victims of Japanese military sexual violence in China: Exploring the meaning of victims' 'desire to speak out' [spitting out what smolders in my heart]), *Chugoku joseishi kenkyu* (Chinese women's history studies), 11.

Iwasa, Jun (1966), *Hyogo: Fusetsu nijunen* (Hyogo: A twenty-year ordeal), Hyogo Shimbunsha.

Kakita, Hajime (2016), 'Fan ni yoru fanzo: 1937-nen no "Takarazuka" kikanshi de no tozaizessen wo kiten ni' (Images of fans, by fans: Using the war of words in the 1937 'Takarazuka' bulletin as a starting point), in Kunimitsu Kawamura (ed.), *Tokushu: Kakita Hajime no shigoto* (The work of Hajime Kakita), *bunka/hihyo* (*Cultures/critiques*), special spring issue, International Japanese Studies Association.

Kanagawa, Megumi (2012), 'Boshi oyobi kafufukushiho seiritsu made no rekishiteki keii' (Debates regarding acts on welfare of mothers with dependents and widows in Japan), *The Wakayama Economic Review*, 370, Wakayama University Faculty of Economics.

Kano, Mikiyo (2007), '"Konketsuji" mondai to tanitsuminzokushinwa no seisei' (The problem of 'mixed-race children' and the growth of monoethnic myths), in Keisen University's Institute for Peace and Culture (ed.), *Senryo to sei: seisaku, jittai, hyosho* (Occupation and sex: Policy, reality and representation), Impact Shuppankai.

Kano, Mikiyo (2017), '"Teikoku no ianfu" to "teikoku no haha" to' ('Imperial comfort women' and 'imperial mothers'), in Toyomi Asano, Kizo Ogura and Masahiko Nishi (eds.), *Taiwa no tameni: 'eikoku no ianfu' to iu toi wo hiraku* (For dialogue: Broaching the question of 'imperial comfort women'), CraneBook.

Kanzaki, Kiyoshi (1974), *Baishun: Ketteiban Kanzaki repoto* (Prostitution: Kanzaki report, definitive edition), Gendaishi Shuppan Kai.

Kasama, Chinami (2012), 'Senryokinihon no shofuhyosho "bebi-san" to "panpan": danseishutai wo kochiku suru baitai' ('*Baby-san*' and '*panpan*' representations of prostitutes in occupied Japan: A medium for promoting male dominance), in Chinami Kasama (ed.), '*Akujo'to 'ryojo' no shintaihyosho* (Physical representations of 'bad girls' and 'good girls'), Seikyusha.

Kawakita, Jiro (1967), *Hassoho: sozoseikaihatsu no tame ni* (The idea method: For developing creativity), Chuko Shinsho.

Kawakita, Jiro (1970), *Zoku hassoho: KJ ho no tenkai to oyo* (Sequel to the idea method: Development and application of the KJ method), Chuko Shinsho.

Keio University Social Work Research Group (ed.) (1953), *Gaisho to kodomotachi: Tokuni kichi Yokosuka-shi no genjo bunseki* (Street prostitutes and children: Focusing on the situation at Yokosuka Base), included in *Nihon (kodomo no rekishi) sosho* (Japan [children's history] series) (1998), Kyuzansha.

Kelly, Liz (1987), 'The continuum of sexual violence' in Jalna Hanmer and Mary Maynard (eds.), *Women, Violence and Social Control*, Palgrave Macmillan.

Kelly, Liz (2001), 'Seiboryoku no renzokutai' (The continuum of sexual violence), Kita Kamiyo (trans.), in Jalna Hanmer and Mary Maynard (eds.), *Jenda to boryoku: Igirisu ni okeru shakaigakutekikenkyu* (Women, violence and social control), Tsutsumi Kaname (trans.), Akashi Shoten.

Kosaka, Kazuya (1990), *Meido in okyupaido Jyapan* (Made in occupied Japan), Kawade Shobo Shinsha.

Kruger, Josiane (2007), *Bosshu no ko: Nachisudoitsuhei to Furansujin to no aida ni umarete* (Boche's children: Born to Nazi fathers and French mothers), Kimie Ozawa (trans.), Shodensha. (Translation of the French, *Née d'amours interdites : Ma mère était française, mon père, soldat allemand*, published by Perrin in 2006.)

Lardreau, Suzanne (2010), *Hokori takai shojo* (Proud girls), Kimie Ozawa (trans.), Ronsosha.

Ministry of Education Research Bureau (ed.) (1962), *Nihon no seicho to kyoiku: kyoiku no tenkai to keizai no hattatsu* (Japan's growth and education: The development of education and economic development), Imperial Society for Local Administration

Ministry of Health, Labour and Welfare (2010), *Heisei 21 nen jinkodotaitokei kakuteisu jokan konin nenji sei nenreibetsu jinko* (Overview of 2009 official demographic statistics part 1: Married population by year, sex and age), data gathered from e-Stat, the portal site of Official Statistics of Japan.

Ministry of Health, Labour and Welfare (2017), *Heisei 28 nendo jinkodotaitokei tokushuhokoku 'konin ni kansuru tokei'no gaikyo* (Overview of 2016 demographic statistic special report 'Marriage statistics').

Miyanishi, Kaori (2012), *Okinawa gunjin tsuma no kenkyu* (Research on Okinawan military wives), Kyoto University Academic Press.

Mühlhäuser, Regina (2015), *Senjo no sei: Dokusosenka no Doitsuhei to joseitachi* (Sex and the Nazi soldier: Violent, commercial and consensual encounters during the war in the Soviet Union, 1941-45), Toshiko Himeoka, Kae Ishii, Takuya Onodera, Yoshie Mitobe and Misachi Wakabayashi (trans.), Iwanami Shoten.

Mühlhäuser, Regina, (2020), *Sex and the Nazi Soldier: Violent, Commercial and Consensual Encounters During the War in the Soviet Union, 1941-45*, Jessica Spengler (trans.), Edinburgh University Press. (Translation of the German, *Eroberungen: Sexuelle Gewalttaten und intime Beziehungen deutscher Soldaten in der Sowjetunion, 1941-1945* published by Hamburger Edition in 2010.)

Mun, Ok-ju and Machiko Morikawa (compilation and commentary) (1996), *Biruma sensen: tateshidan no 'ianfu' datta watashi* (The Burma front: I was one of the 55th Division's 'comfort women'), Nashinoki sha.

Nakamura, Masako (2007), 'Nikkei Amerikajin heishi to Yoroppajin "sensohanayome": Amerikan orientarizumu to howaitonesu' (Japanese-American soldiers and European 'war brides': American orientalism and whiteness), The Japanese Association for American Studies (ed.), *The American Review*, 41.

Nara no Josei Seikatsu shi Hensan Iinkai (ed.) (1995), *Hana hiraku: Nara no josei sekatsu shi* (Blooming: A history of women's lives in Nara), Nara prefecture.

Narita, Ryuichi (2018), 'Seiboryoku to Nihonkindairekishigaku: "deai" to "deaisokone"' (Sexual violence and modern Japanese history: 'Encounters' and 'missed encounters'), in Chizuko Ueno, Shinzo Araragi and Kazuko Hirai (eds.), *Senso to seiboryoku no hikakushi e mukete* (Toward a comparative history of war and sexual violence), Iwanami Shoten.

Nishikawa, Yuko (2013), 'Zoku "Koto no senryu": bokyaku ni koshite' (Sequel to 'The old capital under occupation': Resisting oblivion), in Chubu University (ed.), *Arena*, 15, Fubaisha.

Nishikawa, Yuko (2017), *Koto no Senryo: seikatsushi kara miru Kyoto 1945-1952* (The old capital under occupation: Kyoto's life history from 1945–1952), Heibonsha.

Nishimura, Sei (2015), *Beiguni ga mita senryoka Kyoto no 600 nichi* (A US military doctor's 600 days in occupied Kyoto), Fujiwara Shoten.

Ohara, Kimiko (1972), 'Dai 3 sho, joseikaihoundo no kako, genzai, mirai 2 sengo: Burujoateki "byodo" no moto de' (Chapter 3, The past, present and future of the woman's liberation movement 2 post-war: Under a bourgeois 'equality'), in Kimiko Ohara, Sanae Shiobara and Osamu Ando, *Joseikaiho to gendai: Marukusushugijoseiron nyumon* (Women's liberation and modernity: Introduction to Marxist feminism), San-Ichi Publishing Inc.

Ohara, Kimiko, Sanae Shiobara and Osamu Ando (1972), *Joseikaiho to gendai: Marukusushugijoseiron nyumon* (Women's liberation and modernity: Introduction to Marxist feminism), San-Ichi Publishing Inc.

Ohishi, Sugino (2004), *Bajinia Oruson monogatari: Nihon no kango no tame ni ikita Amerikajinjosei* (The Virginia Ohlson story: An American woman who lived to nurse in Japan), Hara Shobo.

Okada, Taihei (2017), 'Senryoki Nihon no sekkusu waka ni tsuite: katari to aimaisa wo meguru kosatsu' (Sex workers in occupied Japan: Reflections on narrative and ambiguity), in Kei Hibino and Michiko Shimokobe (eds.), *Amerikan reiba: gasshukoku ni okeru rodo no bunkahyosho* (American labor: Cultural representations of labor in the United States), Sairyusha.

Okada, Yasuhiro (2011), 'Senryoka no Nihon ni okeru Amerika kokujinbutai wo meguru jinshu to jenda no poritikkusu: Kyanpu Gifu no dai 24 hoheirentai wo chushin ni' (Race, gender, and African American units in Japan under U.S. military occupation: Focusing on the 24th infantry regiment stationed at Camp Gifu), *Kinjo Gakuin University Journal of Social Science*, 7(2), Kinjo Gakuin University Editorial Committee.

Onodera, Takuya (2017), '"Senjo no sei" honyaku wo oete' (After translating 'Sex and the Nazi Soldier'), *Bulletin of the Association for Modern and Contemporary Western Historical Studies*, 31.

Osa, Shizue (2013), '"CITY MAP OF KYOTO" wo "Yomu": Senryoki kenkyu joron' ('Reading' the 'CITY MAP OF KYOTO': Introduction to Occupation era studies), in Chubu University (ed.), *Arena*, 15, Fubaisha.

Pratt, Mary L. ([1992] 2007), *Imperial Eyes: Travel Writing and Transculturation*, revised 2nd edition, Routledge.

Roberts, Mary L. (2013), *What Soldiers Do: Sex and the American GI in World War II France*, Chicago Press.

Roberts, Mary L. (2015), *Heishi to sekkusu: Dainijisekaitaisenka no Furansu de beihei wa nani wo shitanoka?*(What Soldiers Do: Sex and the American GI in World War II France), Fumika Sato and Miki Nishikawa (trans.), Akashi Shoten.

Ryo Suzuki Seminar, College of Social Sciences, Ritsumeikan University (1991), *Senryoka no Kyoto* (Kyoto under occupation), Bunrikaku.

Saibara, Rieko (2016), *Darin wa 71 sai* (Darlin is 71), Shogakukan.

Sams, Crawford F. (1998), *Medic: The Mission of an American Military Doctor in Occupied Japan and Wartorn Korea*, edited, with an introduction and notes by Zabelle Zakarian, Routledge.

Sata, Ineko (1983), '"Fujinminshu Shimbun" shukusatsuban no kanko ni tsuite' (On the publication of the pocket edition of the 'Women's democratic newspaper'), *Fujinminshu shimbun shukusatsuban (shuseiban) Dai 1 kan 1946-1951)* (Women's democratic newspaper revised pocket edition [vol. 1, 1946–1951]), Fujinminshu Club.

Sato, Fumika (2018), 'Senso to seiboryoku: katari no seitosei wo megutte' (War and sexual violence: On narrative legitimacy), in Chizuko Ueno, Shinzo Araragi and Kazuko Hirai (eds.), *Senso to seiboryoku no hikakushi e mukete* (Toward a comparative history of war and sexual violence), Iwanami Shoten.

Sawa, Ryuken, Tatsuya Naramoto and Mitsukuni Yoshida (eds.) (1984), *Kyoto daijiten* (Kyoto encyclopedia), Tankosha Publishing.

Senba, Goro (1953), 'Jitsudan ni idomu gyomintachi' (Fisherman who handled live ammunition), in Kozo Inomata, Kihachiro Kimura and Ikutaro Shimizu (eds.), *Kichi Nihon* (Base Japan), Wakosha.

Shimizu, Ikutaro, Seiichi Miyahara and Shozaburo Ueda (1953), *Kichi no ko: Kono jijitsu wo dou kangaetara yoi ka* (Base children: How should we think about this fact?), Kobunsha.

Shukan Asahi (ed.) (1995), *Sengo nedanshi nenpyo* (Chronological history of postwar prices), Asahi Bunko.

Sugiyama, Akiko (1988), 'Haisen to RAA' (Defeat and RAA), *Joseigaku nenpo* (Annual report of women's studies), 9, The Women's Studies Society of Japan.

Sunamoto, Fumihiko, Osamu Oba, Hiroyuki Tamada, Satoru Kaku, Joji Osada and Shihori Murakami (2016), 'Senryoki no Okayama ni okeru jutakusesshu ni tsuite: senryoka Nihon no toshi, jyutaku ni kansuru kenkyu sono 3' (House requisition in Okayama in occupied Japan: Research into Japanese cities and housing under the Occupation, part 3), in Architectural Institute of Japan (ed.), *Summaries of Technical Papers of Annual Meetings of the Architectural Institute of Japan*, Architectural Institute of Japan.

Suzuki, Seijun (2010), '"Yopan" to "norainu" to jidoshoju' ('*Panpan*', 'stray dogs' and automatic rifles), in Inuhiko Yomota (ed.), *Suzuki Seijun 'essei korekushon'* (Seijun Suzuki 'essay collection'), Chikuma Bunko.

Svoboda, Terese (2011), *Senryoki no Nihon: aru beigunkenpeitaiin no shogen*, Akiko Okuda (trans.), Hiroshima joseigaku kenkyujo. (Translation of *Black Glasses Like Clark Kent: A GI's Secret from Postwar Japan*, published by Graywolf Press in 2008.)

Taiheiyo Senso Kenkyukai (ed.) (2006), *Kaitei shinpan zusetsu: Amerikagun ga satsuei shita senryoka no Nihon* (Revised and illustrated new edition: Occupied Japan photographed by US Forces), Kawade Shobo Shinsha.

Takemae, Eiji (1983), *GHQ*, Iwanami Shoten.

Takenaka, Katsuo and Etsuji Sumiya (eds.) (1949), *Gaisho, Jittai to sono Shuki* (Streetwalkers: Reality and personal accounts), Yuukosya.

Takushi Crissey, Etsuko (2017), *Okinawa's GI Brides: Their Lives in America*, Steve Rabson (trans.), University of Hawai'i Press.

Tamada, Hiroyuki (2013), 'Senryogun ni yoru sesshujutaku to sesshushisetsuchizu no kenchikushiteki bunseki' (An architectural historical analysis of houses requisitioned by occupying forces and maps of requisitioned facilities), Chubu University (ed.), *Arena*, 15, Fubaisha.

Tamura, Keiko (2002), 'Senryoka ni okeru deai kara kekkon made: sensohanayome to rekishiteki haikei' (From encounters during the Occupation to marriage: War brides and historical background), in Kaori Hayashi, Keiko Tamura and Fumiko Takatsu, *Sensohanayome: kokkyo wo koeta onnatachi no hanseiki* (War brides: Half a century of women who crossed borders), Fuyo Shobo Publishing.

Tanaka, Masakazu (2011a), 'Hajimeni' (Introduction), in Masakazu Tanaka and Toru Funayama (eds.), *Contakuto zon no jinbungaku dai 1 kan Problematique / mondaikei* (Humanities in the contact zone, volume 1: Problematique/problematic), Koyo Shobo.

Tanaka, Masakazu (2011b), 'Contakuto zon to shite no senryoki Nippon: "kichi no onnatachi" wo megutte' (Occupied Japan as a contact zone: Regarding 'women of the base'), in Masakazu Tanaka and Toru Funayama (eds.), *Contakuto zon no jinbungaku dai 1 kan Problematique / mondaikei* (Humanities in the contact zone, volume 1: Problematique/problematic), Koyo Shobo.

Thomas, Lucius G., Lt. Col. M.C. Chief Preventive Medicine, "Venereal Disease Control, Reasons for Nonconcurrence," 13 Nov. 1947, RG331/E1851/9370 part2

Tomiyama, Ichiro (2002), *Boryoku no yokan: Iha Fuyu ni okeru kiki no mondai* (Premonitions of violence: Critical issues according to Iha Fuyu), Iwanami Shoten.

Tomiyama, Ichiro (2013), *Nagaretsuki no shiso: 'Okinawamondai' no keifugaku* (Influx of thought: The genealogy of the 'Okinawa problem'), Impact Shuppankai.

Uchida, Shizue (ed.) and Yayoi Art Museum (2005), *Jogakusei techo: Taisho, Showa otome raifu* (Schoolgirl notebooks: Maiden life in the Taisho and Showa eras), Kawade Shobo Shinsha.

Ueno, Chizuko ([1998] 2012), *Nashonarizumu to jenda* (Nationalism and gender), Iwanami Shoten.

Ueno, Chizuko (2017a), 'Johoseisansha ni naru 9: shitsutekijoho no bunseki to wa nani ka?' (Becoming a producer of information 9: What is qualitative information analysis?), *Gekkan Chikuma* (Monthly Chikuma), 558, Chikuma Shobo.

Ueno, Chizuko (2017b), '"Teikoku no ianfu" no posutokoroniari-zumu' (Post-colonialism and 'imperial comfort women'), in Toyomi Asano, Kizo Ogura and Masahiko Nishi (eds.), *Taiwa no tameni: 'teikoku no ianfu'to iu toi wo hiraku* (For dialogue: Broaching the question of 'imperial comfort women'), CraneBook.

Ueno, Chizuko (2018), 'Senso to seiboryoku no hikakushi no shiza' (Comparative historical perspectives on war and sexual violence), in Chizuko Ueno, Shinzo Araragi and Kazuko Hirai (eds.), *Senso to seiboryoku no hikakushi e mukete* (Toward a comparative history of war and sexual violence), Iwanami Shoten.

Ueno, Chizuko (suprv.), Shigeko Ichinomiya and Toshimi Chazono (eds.) (2017), 'Katari no bunseki: (sugu ni tsukaeru) Uenoshiki shitsuteki bunsekiho no jissen' (Applying the Chizuko Ueno analysis method to oral narrative material [for immediate use]), *Report 27 of the Institute of Ars Vivendi*, Institute of Ars Vivendi, Ritsumeikan University. Available on the homepage of the Institute of Ars Vivendi at Ritsumeikan University (see 'Website' section below).

Ueno, Chizuko, Shinzo Araragi and Kazuko Hirai (2018), 'Hajimeni' (Introduction), in Chizuko Ueno, Shinzo Araragi and Kazuko Hirai (eds.), *Senso to seiboryoku no hikakushi e mukete* (Toward a comparative history of war and sexual violence), Iwanami Shoten.

Yamamoto, Meyu (2013), 'Chichi no konseki: hikiageenjojigyo ni kokuin sareta seiboryoku to "konketsu" no kihi' (Traces of the father: Sexual violence in the repatriation assistance business and avoiding 'mixed blood'), *Teikokunihon no senjisei boryoku: jisedai kenkyu 110* (Wartime sexual violence in Imperial Japan: Next generation research 110), Kyoto University Global COE Program, 'Global Center of Excellence for the Reconstruction of the Intimate and Public Spheres in 21st Century Asia'.

Yamane, Miki (2017), 'Omoni ga utau Takeda no komoriuta: kaishinchiku no "okachan" to no deai' (Mothers singing 'Takeda Lullaby': Meetings with 'mum' in reform districts), in Miki Yamane Editorial Committee (ed.), *Omoni ga utau Takeda no komoriuta: zainichichosenjinjosei no manabi to posutoshokuminchimondai* (Mothers singing 'Takeda Lullaby': What Korean women in Japan learned and the postcolonial problem), Impact Shuppankai.

Yasutomi, Shigeyoshi (2005a), 'Senryoka no Nihon to shinchugun' (Occupied Japan and occupying forces), in Shigeyoshi Yasutomi and Kazuko Stout Umezu, *Amerika ni watatta sensohanayome: Nichibeikokusaikekkon paionia no kiroku* (War brides who travelled to America: Records of pioneers of Japanese-American marriages), Akashi Shoten.

Yasutomi, Shigeyoshi (2005b), 'Nikkeishakai to sensohanayome' (Nikkei society and war brides), in Shigeyoshi Yasutomi and Kazuko Stout Umezu, *Amerika ni watatta sensohanayome: Nichibeikokusaikekkon paionia no kiroku* (War brides who travelled to America: Records of pioneers of Japanese-American marriages), Akashi Shoten.

Yomota, Inuhiko (ed.) (2010), *Suzuki Seijun 'essei korekushon'* (Seijun Suzuki 'essay collection'), Chikuma Bunko.

Yoshimi, Yoshiaki and Myong-suk Yun (1996), 'Shiryo shokai Nihon keisatsu no "ianfu" seisaku 2: "keisatsushi" ni miru "senryogun ianfu", "gun ianfu", "jigyojo ianfu"' (Document introduction, Japanese police 'comfort women' policy 2: 'Occupying army comfort women', 'army comfort women' and 'workplace comfort women' in 'police history'), *The Report on Japan's War Responsibility*, 14 (winter issue).

Newspapers and magazines

Asahi Graph, nos. 8 and 9 of 1957, combined publication of 4 August 1957.

Asahi shimbun (Osaka edition), 1 August 1945 to 31 December 1957.

Asahi shimbun (Tokyo edition), 1 August 1945 to 31 December 1957, 19 January 2010.

Fujin minshu shimbun (Women's democratic newspaper), 24 June 1948.

Kobe shimbun, 1 August 1945 to 31 December 1950.

Kyoto shimbun, 3 April 2015.

The Hankyoreh (Japanese edition), 20 January 2017.

Yomiuri shimbun (Tokyo edition), 1 August 1945 to 31 December 1957.

GHQ materials

Agent Report, 1 May 1950, RG331/SCAP/Box 9894 (c)

Agent Report, 15 June 1950, RG331/SCAP/Box 9894 (c)

Goodrich Lt Col. Inf. Commanding, Guinn B, 1949, 'Military Police Activities in Beppu City, Oita Prefecture', 1 April 1949, RG331/ SCAP/9336

I Corps Engr., Repro., Plant 1259D, 1949, City Map of Kyoto: Kyoto Prefecture, Honshu Japan, 2nd ed., Kyoto Prefectural Library and Archives

Weekly Summary of Events, 19 May 1950, RG331/SCAP/Box 9894 (c)

Weekly Summary of Events, 10 June 1950, RG331/SCAP/Box 9894(c)

Weekly Summary of Events, 7 July 1950, RG331/SCAP/Box 9894(c)

Weekly Summary of Events, 5 August 1950, RG331/SCAP/Box 9894(c)

Websites

Ministry of Health, Labour and Welfare (2017), *Heisei 28-nendo jinkodotaitokei tokushuhokoku 'konin ni kansuru tokei' no gaikyo* (Overview of 2016 demographic statistics special report 'Marriage statistics'), http://www.mhlw.go.jp/toukei/ saikin/hw/jinkou/tokusyu/konin16/index.html (viewed 1 March 2018).

Salary Efficiency Promotion Investigative Team in the Civil Service Department, Local Government Administration Bureau, Ministry of Internal Affairs and Communications, results of a 1 April 2015 fact-finding survey into salaries of local civil servants: http://www.soumu.go.jp/main_sosiki/ jichi_gyousei/c-gyousei/kyuuyo/pdf/h27_kyuyo_1_03.pdf (viewed 16 March 2017).

Seiroka kokusai daigaku no ayumi (History of St. Luke's International University), http://www.luke.ac.jp/about/history.html (viewed 1 June 2017).

Ueno, Chizuko (supervisor), Shigeko Ichinomiya and Toshimi Chazono (eds.) (2017), 'Katari no bunseki: (sugu ni tsukaeru) Uenoshiki shitsuteki bunsekiho no jissen' (Applying the Chizuko Ueno analysis method to oral narrative material [for immediate use]), http://www.ritsumei-arsvi.org/ publications/index/type/center_reports/number/27

Index

Terms

Personal Names

www.ingramcontent.com/pod-product-compliance
Lightning Source LLC
Chambersburg PA
CBHW040254290326
41929CB00051B/3373